HADLEY

CORATO (4) in the English Channel, March 1986, with the Australian built catamaran OUR LADY PATRICIA for Isle of Wight service

(FotoFlite)

HADLEY

W. J. Harvey

By the same author:
        Head Line
        Stena 1939 – 1989
        Empire Tugs
            (with K. Turrell)

ISBN 0.905617.83.5

Edited by David Burrell
Published by World Ship Society, P.O. Box 706, Gravesend, Kent DA12 5UB
Typeset by Highlight Type Bureau Ltd, 2 Clifton Villas, Bradford BD8 7BY
Printed by The Amadeus Press Ltd, 517 Leeds Road, Huddersfield HD2 1YJ

The last thirty years have witnessed a massive contraction of British shipping, virtually obliterating the tramp owner for so long the mainstay of the bulk trades. One of the few survivors is the Hadley Shipping Company Ltd, a company which has for long caused confusion in the minds of casual observers. Was it a Houlder company or not? Houlder colours adorned some ships and Houlder crews were noted on board.

The Hadley Shipping Company has never been a Houlder subsidiary, although having close associations. Their existence is a reminder of a practice permitted by Sir Christopher Furness in Furness, Withy and Company, with whom Houlder Brothers became associated in 1911, whereby directors and senior managers operated their own businesses or fleet, provided excessive time was not taken from their Furness Withy duties and they channelled their insurance, chartering and other needs through Furness Withy offices.

Although Hadley Shipping were incorporated in 1926, roots can be traced to December 1912 when two directors of Houlder Brothers, Maurice C. Houlder and Walter C. Warwick, incorporated The Immingham Agency Company Ltd, to trade in coal and provide agency services to ships calling at Humber ports. Their fellow directors were Sydney H. Kaye and J.P. Harper of Kaye, Son and Company Ltd.

Sydney Kaye's father, Fred Kaye, had been a Houlder employee and expert in the cattle trade from the Plate. With the introduction of refrigeration he persuaded Turner, Brightman and Company to convert their ships for the carriage of frozen meat. Leaving Houlder Brothers in 1893 Fred Kaye established his own firm, but maintained a close association with his old employers in the Plate trade, whilst managing the steamers of the River Plate Fresh Meat Company. The Prince Line Plate agency in London followed. Kaye, Son and Company Ltd became shipowners in 1912 and strengthened their links with Houlder Brothers in 1918 when a substantial shareholding was taken by Furness, Withy and Company and the Royal Mail Steam Packet Company.

The Immingham Agency office was moved from Immingham to Grimsby during 1917 and soon afterward was closed upon the call-up to the colours of the manager (Mr. C. Wilden) for military service. Work was then handled, when required, by the Hull office of Houlder Brothers. In 1922, with the postwar recession, the absence of any prospect of early development of business was noted, but instead of winding up the undertaking it was left to tick along as the Company might serve some useful purpose in the future.

Maurice Charles Houlder.

Born in 1871, Maurice Houlder, son of Edwin Savory Houlder the founder of Houlder Brothers and Company, served his apprenticeship with Amos and Smith in Hull. He subsequently was appointed Marine Superintendent before being elected to the Board of Houlder Brothers in 1901 and Houlder Line the following year. 1901 also saw his appointment to the Committee of Management of the Thames Nautical Training College (HMS WORCESTER).

He became a member of the Baltic Exchange in 1911 and for many years was a member of the Executive Council of the Shipping Federation and a member of the General Committee of the British Corporation Register until it's merger with Lloyd's Register in 1949. He also held directorships of other companies within the Houlder Group until his death, aged 86, in 1957.

Walter Curry Warwick.

Walter Warwick, born in 1878, was destined to spend some 66 years in the shipping industry. That career began in 1896 upon his joining Furness, Withy and Company as assistant to his brother-in-law Frederick Lewis, later the 1st Lord Essendon.

In 1911 Furness Withy acquired a large shareholding in Houlder Brothers and Company and he was appointed Managing Director. Two years later he became a member of the Baltic Exchange and through his sheer ability established himself in high esteem in the shipping fraternity.

He subsequently was appointed Chairman of Royal Mail Lines; Pacific Steam Navigation Company; Shaw, Savill & Albion Company, and Houlder Brothers and Company. Other appointments included membership of the Port of London Authority, Council of the Chamber of Shipping of the U.K. British Liner Committee and the London General Shipowners Society. He retired from the Chairmanship of Shaw Savill in 1947 and from Royal Mail Lines and Pacific Steam during 1960. He relinquished all his remaining business appointments in January 1962, and died at home in Hadley Wood, at the age of 85, early in 1963, having, during his career, served on the Boards of over 50 companies.

Apart from bunkering and a sales agency for the Donnington Main Coal Company Ltd, the principal coal trade was a 25% share in the supply of various Patagonian meat packaging plants, Houlder Brothers also taking 25% and Kaye, Son and Company the balance of 50%. Sales varied from 1,700 tons about 1920 to 8,000 after World War II. For much of the period Welsh and English coal was shipped, until World War II forced them to turn to South African sources. In 1921 an order for 2,500 tons was shipped from Hampton Roads due to a prolonged miners' strike in Britain. Regrettably BEACON GRANGE, chartered for this shipment, went aground on the 6th September 1921 approaching Rio Gallegos, the discharge port, and became a total loss. Regular buyers of these coal shipments included Swift and Company Ltd (San Julian and Rio Gallegos), Armour and Company Ltd (Santa Cruz) and the Deseado Frigorifico.

BEACON GRANGE   *(WSPL)*

A reversal of role occurred during the General Strike of 1926. Instead of shipping coal outwards, Immingham Agency Company acted as agents for ships arriving in the Humber with foreign supplies to alleviate the shortage caused by the strike bound British pits.

The General Strike of 1926.

In the Great War, trade unions progressed in obtaining better conditions for workers, but the return of peace and a Government policy of deflation, keeping sterling on the gold standard and re-introducing pre-war rates of exchange led to wage cuts, longer hours and unemployment. In 1925 mine owners insistence on pay cuts and longer hours led to the General Strike which commenced with a lock-out to enforce their terms. The unions reacted with a call for a general strike to commence on 4th May 1926. Lack of unity amongst the unions saw the strike collapse on the 12th May, apart from the miners who continued to fight until November before being driven back to work by starvation.

With no British exports other countries increased output, and many markets never fully returned to British coal. Such is the consequence of strike action, seen time and time again. Much later the 1966 British seamen's strike allowed operators like Sea-Land to enter trades which have never been recovered by British operators.

The effect on the British economy was drastic. Coal output and usage in 1925 and 1926 was:-

	1925	1926
Industrial, domestic	175,894,116	84,491,136
Exports	50,817,118	20,596,571
Bunkers	16,435,646	7,587,593
Total production	243,146,880	112,675,300 tons.

Factories went on short time for lack of fuel, unemployment rose, the steel industry was unable to maintain supplies and shipyards stopped work for lack of materials. Total tonnage of import and export cargo fell from 124 million tons in 1925 to 110.3 million tons for 1926.

Although freights rose from 1925 to 1926, this did not compensate for extra costs incurred. The tramp trade balanced the 50 million tons of coal exported in 1925 with imports of grains, timber, ore and other bulk cargo. Half of the trade vanished. Imports fell by 3.25 million tons of timber and ore, but an extra 20 million tons of coal joined the inbound flow. To handle this foreign chartering was needed and freights rose. Owners were left with reduced earnings and little changed expenses.

Liners usually sailed from Britain less than full, but arrived back with full cargo. For example Manchester Liners, operating to Canada, loaded westbound light and eastbound normally full. They bunkered in Manchester for the return trip using spare deadweight and cleared Canadian ports with full cargo. Bunkering in Canada for both legs of the voyage reduced the deadweight available eastbound, cargo was shut out and reduced earnings. At the same time bunker prices were higher.

Early in 1924 a new business opportunity arose. The French Government decided to dispose of part of it's fleet and a Mr Behr was assembling a group to finance the purchase of the refrigerated steamer GLACIÈRE, for use in the Siberian frozen salmon trade and general trading when not so employed. Immingham Agency and the financier/shipowner Arthur A. Rappoport joined with Mr Behr to take a one-third interest each.

To finance the £10,000 cost of their one-third interest, Immingham

GLACIÈRE.

3,421g. 2,090n. 331.2 x 46.7 x 23.2 feet.
T.3-cyl. by Central Marine Engine Works Ltd, Hartlepool. Bores 25", 41" & 68", stroke 45". 2,200 ihp. 11½ kts.
3.1918: Completed as WAR COUNTRY by Wm Gray and Company Ltd, West Hartlepool (Yard No. 894) for the Shipping Controller (F. & W. Ritson, Sunderland, managers). 1919: Sold to the French Government, renamed GLACIÈRE. 1921: Converted to a refrigerated ship. 1924: Compagnie Maritime des Transports Frigorifiques, Paris. 1933: Sold to the United Baltic Corporation Ltd, London, renamed BALTARA. 1956: Sold to Alfroessa Cia. Nav. S.A., Panama (Kyrtatas Bros, Piraeus), renamed NIFKIL. 3.1960: Sold, for £27,500, to B.I.S.Co and allocated to Metal Industries Ltd for demolition at Rosyth. 15.3.1960: Delivered. 18.3.1960: Work commenced.
A standard class 'C' ship ordered by The Shipping Controller, WAR COUNTRY was employed as a collier before being sold to the French Government in 1919 along with her sister WAR COPPICE. In 1921 both were converted to refrigerated ships for the fish trade from St Pierre and Miquelon, with three compressors cooling 152,000 cubic feet of insulated space. WAR COPPICE was renamed RÉFRIGÉRANT. Both passed to the control of Compagnie Maritime des Transports Frigorifiques in 1924.

Agency, who had a paid up capital of £500, issued the balance of the authorised capital of £5,000 - Houlder Brothers and Kaye, Son and Company each taking £2,000. The balance was obtained as a loan of £5,500, supplied equally by Houlder Brothers and Kaye, Son and Company.

A clause in the sale contract required GLACIÈRE to remain under the French flag. Compagnie Maritime des Transports Frigorifiques was established in Paris to own her and her sister RÉFRIGÉRANT. GLACIÈRE was chartered to and managed by the Immingham Agency Company Ltd and was to be operated as a Houlder Line boat. Problems were experienced in getting good French crews as GLACIÈRE was the only French flag vessel in the fleet, whilst trade was dull and it was impossible to keep her in full employment. So when, less than eighteen months later, Mr Rappoport expressed an interest in buying the Immingham Agency share this first venture into owning came to an end. The sale price of £11,500 showed a small return on the investment.

The move into shipowning by Immingham Agency was seen by W.C. Warwick, and his fellow Furness Withy director Sir John Esplen, as an ideal opportunity to encourage their sons interest in shipping and in 1924 their sons C. Lewis Warwick and W. Graham Esplen were elected directors, M.C. Houlder and S.H. Kaye resigning at the same time and W.C. Warwick becoming chairman.

In 1926 it was heard that the Anglo-Saxon Petroleum Company (Shell) were selling a large number of war built standard tankers, each with a charter back. Wondering what the catch was, Walter Warwick approached Andrew Agnew of Shell who explained the situation to him.

Anglo-Saxon Sale And Charter-Back.

In 1926 the Anglo-Saxon Petroleum Company Ltd (Shell) conceived the idea of selling some of their old tankers to independent owners with a ten year charter. At the time their technical staff were engaged in the design and construction of many new ships and as such lacked the time needed to supervise the soaring operating costs of the older units. It was felt that the small independent owners would be able to control these rising costs to both their own and Shell's advantage.

Averaging about 8,000dwt, the tankers sold were mainly war built vessels approaching ten years of age. Prices were £60 - 70,000, with an 80% credit line for five to ten years at 5% interest. Charter rates were about 6s (30p) monthly per ton for the first five years, then reduced to 5s 6d (27½p). Shell disposed of around 25 vessels through the scheme.

Most went to Norwegian owners, only two British and two German buyers being involved. The scheme gave a strong boost to the Norwegian tanker sector at a time of strong tanker growth, and several Norwegian owners who commenced business with the scheme went on to become major shipowners.

Brokers for the scheme were Davies and Newman Ltd, London, and J.G. Olsen, Christianssand. Davies and Newman were also tanker owners and operators, and sold two of their ships to Norwegian owners at the same time.

The following were the ships sold from the Anglo-Saxon fleet, to Norway except (* to British owners), (++ to German owners), (** to German owners, 1928 to British), (+ to British owners, 1930 to Norwegian)

Shell name	g.r.t./built. and, if renamed, the new name		
1926			
CEPOLIS	5,578/19 *		
1927			
ABSIA	5,218/18 - SALSAAS.	ACASTA	5,259/18
ADNA	5,197/18	AKERA	5,277/18
ANATINA	5,236/18	ANOMIA	5,198/18 -ANDREA.
CAPSA	5,574/19 - NORDHAV.	CARDITA	5,545/19 - CONCORDIA.
CHITON	5,540/19 - HERON.	CLIONA **	5,563/18 - CORATO.
CONUS	5,578/19 - HERBORG.	CORBIS	5,559/18 - GRANLUND.
CRENATULA +	5,563/18 - MARIT.	GOLD SHELL	5,614/16 - WILLY.
LACUNA	5,882/16 - DOVREFJELL.	LAMPAS	5,861/17
LIMICANA ++	5,861/17 - CH.N.KAHAN.	LITIOPA	5,311/17
1928		1929	
MYTILUS	5,717/16	RADIX	6,832/19
1930			
BUCCINUM	5,237/10	EBURNA	4,795/13
MELANIA	5,824/14 - SARITA.	RANELLA	5,590/12
SILVER SHELL	5,605/15 - SOLI.		

To take advantage of this opportunity with Anglo-Saxon, The Hadley Shipping Company Ltd was incorporated, with a capital of £50,000, on 18th December 1926, the promoters being Lewis Warwick and Graham Esplen (later Sir Graham). The name chosen was adopted from Walter Warwick's home, Hadley Wood, near Potter's Bar in Hertfordshire. An office was established at 53, Leadenhall Street, London, within the offices of Houlder Brothers. The vessel purchased from Anglo-Saxon was CEPOLIS,

"Walmar", the residence of W.C. Warwick at Hadley Wood.

The shareholders of the new Company were:-

Sir John Esplen	£8,000.
C. Lewis Warwick	£7,500.
Sir James Caird	£7,500.
Walter Warwick	£7,000.
Graham Esplen	£7,000.
Immingham Agency Company	£6,500.
Houlder Bros and Company	£5,000.
The Airtight Smoke Box Door Syndicate	£2,500.
J. Larkin	£2,500.
John Weir (engineering family)	£2,500.
R.J. Warwick	£ 250.
John Bradshaw	£ 250.
Mrs Edith Bradshaw	£ 250.

completed in 1919 as the 'Z' class tanker WAR JANDOLI. Sold to Anglo-Saxon in 1919 she was renamed CEPOLIS in 1922, a name retained by Hadley after her purchase. The price was £60,000, of which £30,000 was payable on delivery and the remainder over five years in six-monthly instalments.

Sir John Esplen, Bart.

John Esplen served his time with Fawcett, Preston and Company, Liverpool and subsequently with Earle's Shipbuilding and Engineering Company Ltd, Hull, before joining his father William Esplen as a partner in his Liverpool based firm of consulting engineers and naval architects, then restyled as Esplen and Sons Ltd. Whilst in the business he was instrumental in establishing branches in London, Cardiff, New York, Buenos Aires and Monte Video.

During World War 1 he was appointed director of Overseas Ship Purchase within the Ministry of Shipping. In that capacity he contracted for the construction of some 300 vessels abroad, totalling 2 million tons deadweight and costing some £60 million. Unfortunately when the U.S.A. entered the war they requisitioned all but 11 of the vessels under construction in that country. At the end of the war he was responsible for the sale of 'standard' and other Government owned ships.

He was appointed K.B.E. during 1918 and created a Baronet in 1921. He also served as a director of companies such as British and Argentine Steam Navigation Company Ltd; Furness, Houlder Argentine Lines Ltd; Furness, Withy and Company Ltd; Harris and Dixon Ltd; Johnson Line Ltd and the Wallsend Slipway and Engineering Company Ltd. Other appointments included Chairman of Esplen and Sons Ltd, Wm Esplen, Son and Swainston Ltd, and Fiat British Auxiliaries Ltd. As shipowners the Esplen family built a number of ships for charter to American coal interests.

In January 1930 he died at Kensington, aged 66, and was succeeded as Baronet by his only son William Graham Esplen.

CEPOLIS was taken over on the 24th December 1926, immediately commencing the ten year time-charter to her former owners, and was placed under the management of Immingham Agency Company Ltd. Management fees were agreed at £200 per annum, plus 2 ¹/₂ % on all hire money received, whilst Messrs Esplen, Son and Swainston were appointed marine superintendents at a fee of £105 per annum.

*W.G. Esplen (left)
and
C.L. Warwick (right)*

The rate of hire was, as stated, 6s (£0.30p) per ton deadweight per month, for the first five years and 5s 6d (£0.275p) for the second five years. The first voyage showed a trading profit of £2,841 2s 9d, over 105 days, whilst the first financial year of the company, a period of just over thirteen months, produced a total profit of £7,940 7s 11d after tax and interest payments. This return enabled the Company to pay it's first dividend of 5%, free of tax, absorbing £1,792 10s. The policy of the Company in the early years was to strictly conserve their resources, and to limit dividend distribution until all outstanding liabilities were settled.

Her first years with the Company saw CEPOLIS trading between Curacao and the U.K.; San Pedro to Singapore and Japan, thence South Africa and back to the U.K., where she arrived on 31st October 1928.

It was during her visit to South Africa that a letter was received by James Huntly, her Chief Engineer, wherein Sir John Esplen offered him the post of General Superintendent of the Company in succession to J. Hamilton, which, after some deliberation, he accepted. On an annual salary starting at £300, he commenced his new role early in 1929.

James Huntly

James Huntly's sea-going career had begun in 1907 upon completion of his $5^1/_2$ year apprenticeship at General and Marine Engineering Ltd, Glasgow. He secured his first berth as a Junior Engineer with P&O where he worked his way up to Third Engineer, departing the Company in 1912 claiming that promotion was too slow. He then went as Second Engineer on a tramp steamer to South Africa before emigrating to America where he became a machinist with the Southern Pacific Railway in 1913. Disgruntled by the American lifestyle, he returned to England and P&O as senior Fourth Engineer on MANTUA. He then moved around several P&O vessels and was torpedoed twice. He decided to change employers and moved over to Anglo-Saxon Petroleum, being appointed to a converted collier, BERWINDVALE, trading in the Mediterranean. At the end of the war she was laid-up at North Shields.

It was there that Huntly first encountered the Esplen family, owners of the vessel. John Esplen visited the ship to undertake a study to re-convert the vessel into a collier. Huntly became closely involved with Esplen on the project and subsequently sailed as her Chief Engineer when she returned on charter to Berwind-White Coal Mining Company, New York.

Following that and subsequent ventures around Cuban waters he returned to the U.K., where Mr Esplen offered him the Chief Engineer's post on the collier BERWINDMOOR, under construction at Belfast for the Berwindmoor Steam Ship Company Ltd, for charter to Berwind-White. Once again in September 1923, Huntly returned to Cuban waters, remaining there until April 1926. On his return to the U.K., shipping was in the doldrums and he found great difficulty in obtaining employment. However, such was his reputation he was eventually contacted by Esplen's office in Liverpool, to arrange an interview with Sir John Esplen in London. The meeting resulted in Huntly being appointed Chief Engineer, at £33 per month, on CEPOLIS. He joined her at Rouen on the 8th February 1927, relieving her Anglo-Saxon Chief Engineer.

The staffing of the Hadley office in 1929 was very similar to today, involving five people. Graham Esplen and Carl Warwick as managing directors were assisted by J. Hamilton (or his successor J. Huntly) as marine superintendent, Miss Porter and James Chase (later company secretary and director).

In December 1928, the opportunity arose to purchase another former Anglo-Saxon tanker, once again coupled with a long term charter to the Anglo-Saxon Petroleum Company Ltd. The vessel in question was CLIONA, a sistership to CEPOLIS. This vessel at the time of the original Anglo-Saxon sale and charter-back agreement in 1926, had been purchased by German owners. She had been built in 1918 as WAR JEMADAR, for the Shipping Controller and sold to Anglo-Saxon in 1919.

     She was acquired by Hadley, on 7th December 1928, from Deutsche Tankreederei A.G. at a cost of £64,000. To finance her purchase the Company capital was increased by £25,000 to £75,000. Taken over at San Pedro, her new crew being sent out on the LONDON MERCHANT via Philadelphia, the new vessel was renamed CORATO four months later as Anglo-Saxon had retained the name CLIONA for one of their new ships. This set the pattern of using the letter 'C' for the names of future Company vessels, apart from a few exceptions such as hound names utilised for the small coastal tankers. The purchase of CLIONA from Deutsche Tankreederei was one transaction in a complex package involving the Furness Withy Group wherein GALTYMORE 4,565g. /19 of their Johnson Line and COMINO 4,618g. /18 of their Gulf Line were both sold to Deutsche Tankreederei and renamed LISA and DORIS respectively.

     Initially CORATO was registered at Singapore, before being transferred to London registry. The time-charter with Anglo-Saxon was for nine years, the rate of hire being 6s (£0.30p) per ton deadweight per month for the first 3½ years (£2,530 per month), and 5s 6d (£0.275p) for the remaining 5½ years (£2,319 per month). The charter was subsequently extended for one year at the princely rate of 4s (£0.20p) per ton deadweight (£1,687 per month). The profit on her final voyage was recorded at £15 8s 2d daily. It is interesting to note that in terms of today's money (1996) the £60,000 paid for CEPOLIS is the equivalent of about £2 million whilst the time-charter hire rate of 6s (£2,530 monthly) equates to about £79,000 per month.

     CEPOLIS was in the news early in 1929, when she rendered assistance to a Shell tanker. ARGONAUTA 5,142g. /07 had grounded on Jezsarur Island on 1st February. CEPOLIS responded and assisted in the refloating of the casualty five days later. She then towed her into Bombay where ARGONAUTA was drydocked for repairs to bottom damage that took nearly a month to complete. As recorded in the Hadley minute book a year later, the arbitrator under Lloyd's Form of Salvage Agreement, Mr Butler Aspinall, K.C., awarded £5,000 to CEPOLIS for her services although the award was delayed due to the arbitrator's illness. The minute then details the allocation of this sum between the parties concerned.

Such was the involvement of the Warwick and Esplen families in other interests that assistance was occasionally given to these. One such request came during 1929, when James Huntly was approached by Sir John Esplen, who enquired of his knowledge of diesel engines. Sir John had a financial involvement in a new diesel engine designed by W.S. Burn, being built by Richardsons, Westgarth and Company Ltd, Hartlepool.

Huntly, declaring his ignorance of the subject, was requested to go and work on the engine as a mechanic to familiarise himself with it, as it was to be fitted to a new tanker. It was subsequently decided that, because of it's uniqueness, the tanker would be owned by a new Company - The Iranian Tanker Company Ltd. On the Board of this new concern would be W.G. Esplen and C.L. Warwick. Hadley Shipping invested £20,000 in the venture and both the company and IRANIA would be managed through the Immingham Agency Company Ltd.

Having acceded to the 'request', Huntly departed from the office to work on the engine, keeping factory hours, in overalls as a fitter. He subsequently went to sea aboard IRANIA as Purser, to 'keep an eye' on the machinery performance. Her maiden voyage took her from Glasgow to Constantinople (Istanbul), Constantza to Piraeus returning to Constantza to load for Rouen. W.S. Burn was also on board for this maiden voyage. However as time

The Burn Diesel.

As the diesel developed after the Great War, designers sought greater power and better economy. Unlike the double acting (DA) steam engine, the early diesels were single acting (SA), generally running on a 4-stroke cycle (4SC) with blast air injection. Ultimately the 2-stroke (2SC) was to prevail and solid, airless injection proved more economical. In the 1920's DA diesels were introduced to provide greater power, despite the complication of a lower cylinder head and the extremely arduous conditions prevailing inside a compression-ignition engine. The appearance of supercharging allowed a return to SA, avoiding the complications of DA design.

In the Hartlepools, Richardsons, Westgarth and Company Ltd (RW) obtained licences to build Tosi and Doxford diesels. Soon they sought to design their own marque, a task delegated to W.S. Burn, in 1924. He prepared drawings for a 2SCDA engine with solid injection, the prototype of which ran in 1926.

It was to be 1929 before the first unit, of 1,250 bhp went to sea powering IRANIA. The following year a smaller, 1,000 bhp, engine was erected for Ashford power station. This failed to meet the buyer's requirements and was left on RW's hands. Early teething troubles, allied to a dearth of orders for shipyards after the Wall Street collapse in 1929, combined to keep the RW-Burn order book empty until 1935, when the Silver Line motorships SILVERPINE and SILVERLARCH were partially reconstructed and re-engined to meet the needs of their owner's services. The Burn engine was chosen and a 4,000 bhp unit fitted in each ship. The following year the power station engine was converted for marine use and went into ST GERMAIN.

These four units completed the RW production, they henceforth concentrated on the popular Doxford range. However, the North Eastern Marine Engineering Company Ltd later erected two 4,500 bhp Burn engines which, in 1944/45, were installed in the tankers EMPIRE INVENTOR and EMPIRE CHANCELLOR.

Like many other early designs, the Burn never achieved popularity. Being DA introduced complications and some parts were reportedly too heavy. The Burn was soon followed by supercharging and this, allied with the simpler SA design, probably played a major part in it's demise, although had the Great Depression not commenced in 1929, it is likely a few more may have been built.

progressed, following Huntly's return to his office, the story became a sad one. Due to what was thought to be a flaw in the engine design, the ship suffered continual machinery problems and was soon laid up for disposal, eventually finding a Norwegian buyer in 1937. Her new owners ran her for many years and, during that period, suffered little or no problems. They put the earlier troubles down to the inability of the ship's engineers to fully understand the engine's operating characteristics, rather than the engine itself.

A snap view of the 1930 major shareholdings in The Hadley Shipping Company Ltd, was thus:-

Sir James Caird	£14,375.
Sir Graham Esplen	£13,800.
Immingham Agency Company	£ 8,305.
W. C. Warwick	£ 7,987.
Lady Esplen	£ 6,000.
Houlder Brothers	£ 5,750.
Others	£18,783.
Total	£75,000.

(National Maritime Museum)

Sir James Caird, Bt.

Born during 1864 in Glasgow, James Caird commenced his business career in 1878 with Graham & Company, Glasgow, East India merchants. Moving to London in 1889, he soon became manager of Turnbull, Martin and Company.

This concern was founded by James Turnbull in 1867. Their first steamer, SANDRINGHAM, was acquired in 1874. Ten years later ELDERSLIE joined the fleet as the first purpose built steamer for the New Zealand frozen meat trade. Later, in 1904, they formed part of the Federal-Houlder-Shire Line (in 1912 restyled Federal & Shire Line) in the trade from Britain to Australia and New Zealand.

During 1903 Caird had become the sole partner in Turnbull, Martin and Company, selling control to Cayzer, Irvine and Company (Clan Line) in 1910. The same year saw the Elderslie Steam Ship Company Ltd wound up and replaced by the Scottish Shire Line Ltd to which the seven ship fleet was transferred. Clan Line purchased the capital of Scottish Shire Line on the 1st January 1918, although it continued under the management of Turnbull, Martin and Company Ltd, until 1960, when reorganised within the British & Commonwealth Shipping Group.

Caird's association with Turnbull, Martin and Company lasted until 1928. During the Great War he was chairman of the Standard Shipbuilding Company, Chepstow. He gave £65,000 for the restoration of HMS VICTORY, for which he was created a Baronet in 1928. He then defrayed the cost of alterations (£80,000) to the Royal Hospital School on the founding of the National Maritime Museum, Greenwich, and gifted the MacPherson and Mercury collections of prints and ship models (£138,000). Other notable donations followed.

At the time of his death in 1954, following five years of illness, he had served on the Board of no less than 25 companies.

By 1930 Hadley Shipping had amassed sufficient resources to justify placing an order with Hawthorn, Leslie and Company, Newcastle, for the construction of a new tanker of around 5,500 tons deadweight, to be built to a high specification and be suitable for the carriage of clean spirit. The contract price was £80,000, and to assist with the financing of the vessel the Company issued a further 10,150 £1 shares.

It was the original intention that the new vessel be fitted with a diesel but the cost proved excessive and steam was chosen. CERINTHUS, as she was named, was delivered on 20th December 1930, and fixed with a time-charter to the American Texas Oil Company for two years (with an option of a third), at the rate of 9s 6d (£0.475p) per deadweight ton per month, returning a net profit of £12,000 per annum. The vessel proved to be extremely efficient, being off service for only three days and nine hours within the two year charter period. She was commanded for many years by Captain John Fleming Allen, who had joined the fleet as 2nd mate of IRANIA in 1931. Subsequently he was master of CEPOLIS (1934-7), CERINTHUS (1937-8) and JAMAICA PLANTER (1938 - 40) before being appointed Marine Superintendent.

Following the expiration of the Texas charter, CERINTHUS spent much of her time tramping in the lubricating oil and palm oil trades from the U.S.A. and the west coast of Africa respectively. Palm oil cargoes from West Africa were often consigned to J. Bibby and Sons, Liverpool. This was not a destination which had been accepted without careful consideration as CERINTHUS became one of the largest ships to trade into the East Waterloo Dock, Liverpool, her hull only just fitting the entrance lock.

OTTERHOUND   (WSPL)

ELKHOUND. Note dog on funnel

ELKHOUND.

O.N. 161282. 684g. 309n.   177.5 x 31.6 x 11.5 feet. Tanker.
Two, 6-cyl. 4 S.C.S.A. (350 x 350mm) MAN F6V 35/35 type oil engines manufactured
by Motorenwerke Augsburg-Nurnberg, Augsburg, geared to twin screw shafts. 560 bhp.
9¾ kts.
12.6.1929: Launched and 10.1929 completed by Charles Hill and Sons Ltd., Bristol
(Yard No. 173) 10.1931: Reconstruction completed by Grangemouth Dockyard
Company Ltd, Grangemouth.
729g. 301n.   180.5 x 31.6 x 10.2 feet.
T.3-cyl. (14", 23" & 38" x 24") 700 ihp engine manufactured by Aitchison, Blair Ltd,
Clydebank. 9 kts.
In 1929 ELKHOUND was completed by Charles Hill and Sons Ltd, Bristol, for the
Esplen controlled Channel Tanker Company Ltd, London, and was powered by MAN
diesels designed for UB class submarines. The second Esplen coastal tanker she traded
alongside OTTERHOUND. But unlike OTTERHOUND she did not pass to Immingham
Agency management in 1931.

continued over

The fire damaged ELKHOUND at Grangemouth

She had only traded for a year before suffering a severe engine room fire in October 1930. Commanded by Captain Clausen she was about to sail from Thames Haven on 17th October 1930 with 600 tons of benzole when fire broke out. Towed clear by the tugs SUN IV and SUN XII she was taken, in view of possible explosion, down river and beached on Barrow Sand. The following day, when the fire had burnt out, she was towed back to Thames Haven to discharge and was then docked in Green's No.2 dry dock at Blackwall.

Such was the severity of the damage that, even only one year old, repairs were not considered viable and as a result was declared a constructive total loss.

However, on 16th January 1931, the Grangemouth Dockyard Company Ltd purchased her 'as lies' for £3,500 and had her towed to Grangemouth where she arrived on the 29th January. Classed as a 'stand by job' she was taken in hand when other work was short between May and October 1931. In dry dock she was converted from a twin screw motorship into a single screw steamer, work that entailed a major rebuild of her stern with a new stern frame and poop extended forward by 13' 6". Successful sea trials were undertaken on 30th October.

ELKHOUND was then laid up at Grangemouth until 1934 when sold to Kenneth Irving's Irving Oil Company Ltd, St John, N.B. for £17,000. She was placed in the ownership of Irving Steamships Ltd, without change of name, and was employed in their Canadian trade.

Her end came in 1949 after discharge of a cargo at Newcastle, N.B. On 3rd May an explosion took place in No.2 starboard tank followed by fire. Such was the force of the blast a 60 foot section of main deck was thrown onto the river bank. Towed away from the berth she broke in two by way of No.3 tank and sank midstream in the Miramichi River. Her forepart capsized, but her afterpart sat upright with the funnel showing above the water. Refloated and beached on the 9th July, repairs were estimated at $125,000. In view of this and her age, the decision was taken to sell the wreck for demolition where she lay.

The early 1930's was a period of great depression in the shipping industry. Large numbers of ships were laid up and many companies were to go out of business, but Hadley Shipping, with it's two Anglo-Saxon charters and earnings from the new ship, survived and even prospered through the long years of the slump although CERINTHUS, being on the spot market, was laid up on the Tyne between November 1934 and March 1935 for lack of employment. Company dividends were maintained at the 1930 level of 5% until 1934 when increased to a new high of 7.5%, against a profit of £34,499, somewhat pleasing in the light of shipping conditions at the time.

Meanwhile, during 1931, James Huntly had been approached by Lewis Warwick and Graham Esplen regarding Coastal Tankers Ltd, another family business, which had been founded on 25th February 1927 by Sir John Esplen to own the new small tanker OTTERHOUND. She had, for a short period, traded with ELKHOUND owned by another family Company, Channel Tankers Ltd. ELKHOUND however had suffered a disastrous engine room fire in October 1930 and been sold to a Scottish shipbuilder for reconstruction and resale.

This left OTTERHOUND and a company running at a loss. The feasibility of turning the loss into profit was discussed at length by the threesome and after a prolonged debate it was agreed that management of this Company would be accepted into the Hadley Shipping / Immingham Agency office by James Huntly. It is to the credit of Huntly that after only one year under his control the loss had been turned to profit, even if only just.

Late in 1933, as a show of faith in that decision, coupled with a view to diversification, Hadley Shipping decided to enter the coastal tanker market and ordered a new 1,500 tons deadweight vessel. Named BASSETHOUND, reported as being a belated substitute for ELKHOUND, she was destined to complement Coastal Tankers' OTTERHOUND. Delivered on 4th April 1934 at a total cost of £37,995 5s 3d, she entered a very depressed, over tonnaged and unprofitable market which led to periods of idleness and trading off the British coast, as for instance a cargo of whale oil loaded in Labrador for delivery to Copenhagen. By late 1934, however, the shipping market in general was beginning to show some sign of recovery, albeit helped by the activities of the Tramp Advisory Committee. The Schierwater Scheme was having a similar effect on the deep-sea tanker market early in 1935, although there was a still some time to go before there was a consistently sustained improvement in the coastal tanker market. Nevertheless, by the end of 1935, the Directors were able to report that Hadley's loans were ALL paid off.

The Schierwater Scheme.

The tanker market collapsed in 1930, with 15% of the tanker fleet laid up by 1933. The International Tanker Owners Association (INTERTANKO) was formed in 1934 (chaired by H.T. Schierwater) to operate the Oil Tanker Pooling Scheme. Independent tanker owners, with a fleet of some 2.5 million tons deadweight, had about 40% laid up. At this time Hadley were a dedicated tanker company, and at their annual general meeting on 7th April 1931 it was stated '. . . 1931 is outstanding in the Annals of the Shipping Industry as probably the worst on record and many sound, old established Companies have found it necessary to substantially reduce, and in some cases, cease to pay dividends.'

Under the scheme owners with tankers trading paid a percentage of earnings to the Pool, which compensated owners with laid-up ships. Contributions, originally 10% soon rose to 15% on voyage and 18% on time charters. The laid-up allowance paid the first year to owners was £1 15s. 1½ d (£1.76p) per gross ton. Maximum laid-up allowance was originally 48s (£2.40p) per gross ton per annum, reduced to 30s (£1.50p) in 1936 to combat the attraction of speculative building. Increased demand for tankers in 1935, in part due to the Italo-Abyssinian War, saw the levy halved. Further reductions followed, reached a low of 0.75% and 1% in 1937, then rose to 10% and 12.5% in 1938. The levy reacted to the market, laid-up tonnage was 207,574 dwt in December 1936 and freights had improved in 1937. Hadley Shipping both contributed to, and benefited from, the Pooling Scheme.

Success was guaranteed by the attitude of major oil companies, who gave preference to chartering tankers entered in the Pool. Better markets in 1937 reduced the need for the Scheme until conditions fell off in 1938. Finally World War in 1939 completely removed the conditions which gave birth to the Scheme. Later plans for a similar response to adverse conditions never succeeded, due to the strictures of American Anti-Trust legislation.

H.T. Schierwater (1876 - 1952) chaired Intertanko from 1934 until 1949. A Director of United Molasses Company Ltd, he was nominated to the Shipping Defence Advisory Sub-Committee at the Admiralty in 1939. In 1940 he became chairman of the oil tanker section of the Chamber of Shipping (member of Council since 1934), and was nominated Vice-President of the Chamber in 1944 and President for the year 1945/6. At United Molasses he became a Director of Athel line Ltd (formed in 1939) and Tankers Ltd (1921) and Deputy-Chairman of both in 1944. He retired from all three Boards in 1947 and died at Eastbourne on 7th August 1952 in his 76th year.

DEPRESSION TO WAR   *4*

It was reported that during 1935 discussions had been underway for some considerable time with Kaye, Son and Company regarding the possibility of the Company financing the building of a ship for the banana trade. Kaye, Son and Company were managers of the Jamaica Banana Producers Association fleet, and as such were seeking capital for a purpose built vessel. Because of their links with the Kaye family Hadley Shipping had the opportunity to extend their operations into a new sphere of activity.

The Company, after much deliberation, accepted the challenge and placed an order for the fruit carrier with Lithgows Ltd, Port Glasgow. She would have superior accommodation for twelve passengers. The contract price was £152,000. The time-charter was for five years at £2,295 per month, coupled with an option to extend the charter to ten years. A further option was to purchase the vessel after three years, for £132,500, or at a later date at a lower price allowing for depreciation at 5% per annum.   JAMAICA PLANTER, as she was named by Lady Strathcarron on 8th June 1936, became the first motorship to be owned by the Company, delivered in August 1936. Captain Cyril Liam Brien was appointed master. Originally a Blue Star man he had entered the banana trade when he joined Kaye's fleet in 1929 and commanded various of their managed fleet before taking JAMAICA PLANTER between 1936 and 1939.

Unfortunately, somewhere along the line an optimistic or undetected miscalculation resulted in a seriously underpowered vessel that had great difficulty in maintaining the contract speed called for under the terms of the charter. As a result, following much unsuccessful work by onboard engineers it became necessary to dispatch the vessel to the Copenhagen yard of Burmeister and Wain. There between 31st October and 23rd December 1938 the machinery was rigorously tested and costly modification work carried out. Subsequently Lithgows paid a claim for £13,500.

With the delivery of JAMAICA PLANTER, the Company operated a fleet of five vessels consisting of the two former Anglo-Saxon tankers CEPOLIS and   CORATO,   BASSETHOUND,   CERINTHUS   and   JAMAICA PLANTER. In 1935, Hadley Shipping and Coastal Tankers decided that coastal operations should be extended and Hadley Shipping, being the larger partner, time-chartered CORNELIA S, a small tanker under construction for Deutsche Fanto Ges., Hamburg. Ownership was transferred to and the vessel completed for the newly founded Fanto Petroleum and Shipping Company Ltd, London (her German-Jewish owners using her to transfer funds abroad under the tough German exchange control regulations). She was placed under management of Immingham Agency Company during

December 1936 and to undertake the charter it was subsequently decided that she be renamed DAXHOUND in January 1937.

In February 1937, following the completion of her Shell charter, CEPOLIS was sold to Japanese shipbreakers Aoyagi Shosen, Yokohama for £11,000, through Davies and Newman Ltd. CORATO followed her in 1938 but her sale to Japan fell through and she was then sold to T.W. Ward Ltd, Briton Ferry for £10,500.

By 1937/38 the freight market had improved considerably and the Company was able to report nearly doubled profits, £65,000 for 1937, which enabled a special bonus of 2.5% to be paid in addition to the dividend of 7.5%. In April 1938 two new Directors were appointed to the Board, Cyril Warwick, nephew of Chairman Walter Warwick, and James Huntly, the company's Superintendent who, as stated earlier, had started his company career as Chief Engineer on the CEPOLIS. Meanwhile the owners of DAXHOUND had asked to withdraw from the time-charter as they wished to sell her. Hadley Shipping agreed to the request, against a payment of £1,000 compensation. One of the material factors in mind at the time DAXHOUND was chartered was that by running three ships, including Coastal Tankers' OTTERHOUND, the fleet had a greater degree of flexibility. In order to maintain that flexibility following the withdrawal of DAXHOUND, it was decided to purchase a replacement vessel. The Norwegian flag MITRA was inspected, found to meet Company requirements, and purchased. A vessel of some 2,500 tons deadweight, she had been built in Germany in 1931. Costing £41,000 she was delivered to Hadley Shipping in March 1939. Renamed DAXHOUND, she retained a name familiar to the oil fraternity.

It was not long before war was to raise it's ugly head again. At the outbreak of hostilities the fleet stood at five vessels, including Coastal's OTTERHOUND. However, in August 1940, the Jamaica Banana Producers Association exercised their option to purchase JAMAICA PLANTER and she passed to their ownership for £127,903 and the management of Kaye, Son and Company, until becoming a casualty in 1944. In thick fog near the end of a passage from Halifax she collided with the American tanker WELLESLEY anchored in Barry Roads and foundered. BASSETHOUND

OTTERHOUND
(W. Haig Barry)

EMPIRE TAGINDA   (WSPL)

was requisitioned by the Ministry of Shipping (later the Ministry of War
Transport) in August 1940 and was dispatched to Freetown, Sierra Leone,
where she spent over three years on station as a fresh water carrier.
DAXHOUND and OTTERHOUND meanwhile continued to trade around
the coast on charter to the Petroleum Board, whilst CERINTHUS continued
her employment in the palm oil trade from West African ports.

During the war years the Company, in conjunction with Coastal Tankers
and Immingham Agency, managed a considerable fleet of ships on behalf of
the Ministry of War Transport. In total 127 vessels, mainly tankers but
including some general cargo ships, were managed at one time or other,
which placed a considerable burden on the small office staff. James Huntly's
retirement appreciation gives this number, even though it is now impossible
to identify some of them. In 1941, James Huntly was also appointed a
director of Overseas Towage and Salvage Company Ltd.

Not all of the vessels owned or managed were to survive the war, some
becoming victims to enemy action. The first loss was the tanker EMPIRE
AMETHYST which sailed from New Orleans on the 6th April 1942 bound
to Freetown, Sierra Leone, with a cargo of 12,000 tons of spirit. Seen on
12th April some 150 miles south of Haiti she was posted untraced on 24th
June, believed lost on 14th April at a position 16N 72W.   Later it was
ascertained she had been sunk at dawn on 13th April, torpedoed by U 154, in
17.40N 74.50W., with the loss of her entire crew of 47. The Master of
EMPIRE AMETHYST was 44 year old Geoffrey Potter, who had joined
Hadley, as Master of CEPOLIS, in October 1932. Previously a Lieutenant
R.N. he was granted a Merchant Navy 'ticket' in 1924. After CEPOLIS went
for scrap he had BASSETHOUND and CERINTHUS until sent to stand by
the building EMPIRE AMETHYST early in 1941.

THE HADLEY SHIPPING Co., LIMITED.

DIRECTORS.
W. C. WARWICK (CHAIRMAN).
SIR JAMES CAIRD, BT.
SIR W. GRAHAM ESPLEN, BT
JAMES HUNTLY.
CYRIL W. WARWICK.

53, Leadenhall Street,

London. E.C. 3.

8th December, 1942.

Mrs. Read,
49, Dock Road,
Little Thurrock,
GRAYS.

Dear Madam,

s.s. "CERINTHUS"

We very much regret to advise you that this vessel has been lost by enemy action.

We are glad to inform you the Admiralty have advised us that all the crew got away in two lifeboats and, so far, one boat containing half the crew, all well, has been picked up.

Up to the present the names of those picked up are unknown to us but we shall advise you by telegram immediately we have any further news.

Yours faithfully,

For and on behalf of THE HADLEY SHIPPING CO.LTD.

P.S. A telegram has just been received saying your husband has been landed safe and well in West Africa

Director.

Later that year, on 9th November, the Company owned CERINTHUS also became a war loss. She had sailed in ballast from Oban in convoy ON 141 on 25th October, bound for Freetown. Leaving the convoy on 2nd November, she found herself a week later in 12.27N., 27.45W. Shortly before midnight on 9th November a torpedo missed astern, but a second hit the port No.5 tank. Two boats were launched and stood by the ship, but a second torpedo hit and U 128 then surfaced and shelled her for one and a half hours until she sank. The two boats kept together until 17th November when they lost sight of each other in a rain squall. During this time repeated attempts to use the boat radio failed to raise any reply. Chief Officer Hawkins boat was sighted by a Sunderland aircraft on 1st December and later that day, after 22 days adrift, they were picked up by HMS BRIDGEWATER and landed at Freetown on 6th December. The tragedy was the second boat, commanded by Captain Chadwick. It was not sighted until 24th January when only one man was still alive. The sole survivor from this boat was picked up by the American steamer KENTUCKIAN 5,200g./10 and landed at Port of Spain on 31st January. Letters advising the loss were sent out to all next of kin on 8th December 1942, signed by James Huntly on behalf of the company (see example above). It was also on that day that notification was received from The Admiralty of the safe landing of survivors by HMS BRIDGEWATER (see P.S. in letter). Captain James Chadwick, born in Manchester in 1894, was amongst those lost. For many years a master with C.T. Bowring and Company, he had survived the sinking of their CYMBELINE by the raider WIDDER on 2nd September 1940. Taking CERINTHUS in January 1942 he died in the second lifeboat on 10th January 1943, two weeks before it was sighted by the KENTUCKIAN.

Captain T.B. White

In May 1943 Trevor White was dispatched by the Merchant Navy Officers Pool to attend an interview with James Huntly, Chief Superintendent of the Hadley Shipping Company of which, until that time, he had never heard. His initial impression of Huntly was of a dour, non-smoking, teetotal Scot who demanded that everyone be the same in the seafaring profession. He was appointed to EMPIRE FAUN which he joined at Smith's Dock, North Shields. Somewhat taken aback by her diminutive size he was to undertake an initial seventeen month voyage around the Mediterranean ending with the landings in southern France. He later joined EMPIRE GAIN and was to run the gauntlet during the civil war in Greece whilst plying between Augusta (Sicily) and Piraeus. During his time on board, between May 1945 and February 1946, he was caught in a hurricane off the coast of Newfoundland, which whipped up mountainous seas the like of which he had never experienced in all his time at sea. In 1946 he was transferred to the ex-German prize EMPIRE TAGINDA and painstakingly nursed her home from Sierra Leone, stopping several times enroute for major machinery repairs. That voyage from Freetown to London took some six months. In March 1947 he was given his first Command THORNOL, and subsequently remained with the Company commanding the tankers CORATO from her builders and CERINTHUS until November 1959. As Houlder Bros were building tankers Hadley men were transferred and Trevor White was appointed to BIDFORD PRIORY. Having completed 15 years in command Captain White came ashore as Marine Superintendent to succeed Captain Allen and in his new role continued his association with Hadley.

The following year two further managed ships were lost. Pantellaria had surrendered on 11th June 1943, and preparations were in hand for the Allied landings in Sicily (9-10th July). EMPIRE MAIDEN had been in the Mediterranean since March and now, supplying the Allied garrison on Pantellaria, found herself in the front line. Arriving from Sousse on 12th June she grounded and, whilst still aground, came under repeated attack from dive-bombers. Being the only ship in harbour she fortunately only reported near misses. Returning on 14th June a FW190 attack missed astern, sank an MGB, holed and flooded EMPIRE MAIDEN's engine room. Further bombing attacks missed but caused further damage, bursting the bunker bulkheads and buckling her deck and sides. Abandoned Captain McClure and his crew were taken to Sousse on board an LCT and travelled to Algiers from whence they were repatriated to Britain on board the SAMARIA. EMPIRE MAIDEN was refloated on 10-11th June 1948 and repaired at Messina, re-engined with an Italian built compound steam engine and on 7th August 1948, re-entered service as the Italian EMPIRE MAIDEN. This is strange but nevertheless true. She retained and traded under her British name of EMPIRE MAIDEN whilst flying the Italian flag until her further sale and renaming in 1953.

The second 1943 loss was EMPIRE COMMERCE, also in the Mediterranean. Captain Fitzpatrick was ordered to join convoy MKS26 from Bona to Algiers, but having a foul bottom and fuel problems (she had been

CUMBRIA at Venice (Foto d'Antonio)

CERINTHUS (4) in the English Channel (FotoFlite)

CLYMENE (1) at Curacao   *(F. Lott)*

A Christmas message from the crew of COTINGA at Youghal, 1983

The damage to CLYDE BRIDGE in the St Lawrence early in 1972, and proceeding down river through ice

CORATO (4) undergoing conversion at Swansea for the Falklands charter
(FotoFlite)

CLYMENE (2), with Consolidated Bathurst funnel markings, sailing from Helsinki
with a timber cargo *(Studio Magnus Lofving)*

supplied with light gas oil instead of diesel) could only manage 7 knots with torpedo nets streamed. The convoy speed was 11 knots. Falling behind from her station (No.73 - the rear ship in the starboard wing column) the nets were hauled to catch up. At 21:00 hrs on 30th September 1943 a suspicious object was sighted on the starboard quarter. Ten minutes later a torpedo exploded in No.5 tank, starboard side. U 410 had fired a spread of five torpedoes, hitting EMPIRE COMMERCE and FORT HOWE. Damage extended right across the ship, with the aft end slewed 10 degrees to starboard and the port side split right open. The crews of the two ships were shortly picked up by HMS ALISMA. The stern of EMPIRE COMMERCE soon broke off and sank. The forward section, picked up by a tug, was abandoned on fire off Phillipeville, to drift ashore 8 miles east of that town and burn out.

At dusk on the 13th August 1944 the managed RADBURY was on passage from Lourenco Marques for Mombasa when, in 25.00S., 42.30E., two torpedoes fired by U 862 exploded on the starboard side. Survivors landed on Europa Island three days later, failed to attract the attention of a passing Liberty ship on 13th September and were finally sighted by a patrolling Catalina aircraft on 26th October. Two days later they were taken off by HMS LINARIA. Later (14th November) one survivor, cook Sing Kiang Yung, drifted ashore on a raft made from hatch covers, at Quelimane. Chief Engineer Sung Tsu Ten, who had taken charge of the survivors on Europa Island, was appointed an O.B.E. in 1945.

The final loss was the managed tanker ROUSEVILLE which was on a ballast voyage, under command of Captain A.M. Kennedy, from Rouen to Le Havre when, on 26th October 1944, she exploded a mine in the vicinity of Couerval Lighthouse, off Vieux Point in the estuary of the River Seine. The explosion was heard four miles away in Quillebeuf. It ignited a fire in No.1 tank and she was beached on the north shore with her back broken in two places. Abandoned and still on fire, her crew had scarcely reached Quillebeuf when, two hours later, an even more violent explosion saw the wreck largely disintegrate. The crew returned to Britain on board BAILEY FOSTER 1,791g./43, and what little was left of ROUSEVILLE was declared a total loss on 1st November.

The manning of the large fleet of managed ships was a problem. In part this was met by officers who had swallowed the anchor returning to sea. Typical was James Fitzpatrick, an Irishman from Waterford. His last command had been Lamport and Holt's PHIDIAS in 1930. He now took EMPIRE COMMERCE from the builders until she was sunk in a matter of only months later, after which he commanded BASSETHOUND, EMPIRE TADPOLE and WAVE DUKE. Another Irishman, from Islandmagee, was John McClure whose last command had been the tanker BRITISH ENTERPRISE from 1930 - 1932. Returning to sea in December 1939 he joined Hadley in November 1942, taking EMPIRE MAIDEN until bombed and lost in June 1943. Command of further managed ships followed, TITUSVILLE, EMPIRE JEWEL, EMPIRE COPPICE and EMPIRE BAIRN.

POST WAR RECONSTRUCTION 5

The cessation of hostilities in 1945 saw the combined Hadley/Coastal Tankers owned fleet standing at only three coastal ships - DAXHOUND, BASSETHOUND and OTTERHOUND. Some of the managed vessels remained under control for several years after the war, as well as further vessels allocated to their management.

EMPIRE SIMBA and Gas Warfare.

Gas remained a threat throughout World War II. There were only two major instance of it being released, both accidental, when EMPIRE SAILOR was sunk by U 518 on 21st November 1942 and the Bari tragedy of 2nd December 1943.

Large gas munition stockpiles existed in both Allied and Axis hands, in 1945 nearly 300,000 tons being captured in Germany alone. The disposal of this lethal collection was urgent. In 1945 a start was made, some was burnt but over 200,000 tons was loaded on old merchant ships and scuttled at sea in the Skagerrak, Kattegat, Baltic, North Sea, Bay of Biscay and off the Scottish and Irish coasts. Elsewhere ships were scuttled with nerve gases in the Mediterranean, off Sydney, the North American coast, etc.

Between 1945 and 1957, 24 ships loaded at British ports, mainly Barry, South Wales and Cairnryan, Scotland, and were scuttled in deep water. They carried mustard gas, phosgene, sarin, tabun, and other material.

EMPIRE SIMBA, managed by Hadley Shipping since 1941, was the first ship to load at Cairnryan (eleven others followed up to 1957). She sailed on 9th September 1945 with 500,000 mustard gas shells (8,032 tons). Four days later she was scuttled in 1,300 fathoms in position 55.20N 11.00W.

Today with the passage of time, there is increasing concern and anxiety over these gas dumps. The containers and the ships carrying them are rotting and there is little knowledge of the consequences when the gases enter the food chain.

Steps were quickly taken to rebuild the fleet and, in 1946, a Canadian war-built standard cargoship, FORT ST PAUL, was taken on a two year bare-boat charter from the Ministry of War Transport, at £1,150 per month. This was later extended by a further two years at £2,000 per month. In 1947 the war-built Liberty SAMKANSA was purchased for £135,000 and renamed CERINTHUS. Both FORT ST PAUL and CERINTHUS were destined to spend much, if not all, of their time on charter to Houlder Line, operating on their River Plate service. During that period both vessels were painted in Houlder colours.

In 1946 James Huntly, at the age of 59, was approached by John Houlder and his father Maurice Houlder, with the view to his appointment as Chief Superintendent of Houlder Brothers. He subsequently accepted. Together with John Allen, who had in the early war years come ashore to be Huntly's right-

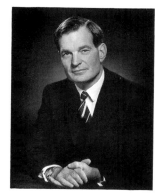

hand man as Marine Superintendent for Hadley Shipping, he moved over to the Houlder Offices. Huntly was subsequently appointed a director of Alexander Shipping Company, Montclare Shipping Company and Ore Carriers Ltd.

SAMEARN, another Liberty ship, was purchased by Claremont Shipping Company (a company owned by John Houlder and Cyril Warwick) and renamed CLAREPARK, passing briefly through the offices of Immingham Agency before reverting to Houlder management. They had managed her during the war on behalf of the Government and were now resuming the task during her charter operation on their River Plate service. Meanwhile the coastal tankers continued to trade, at first on charter to the Petroleum Board and subsequently to various of the major oil companies. Coastal Tankers Ltd began purchase negotiations with the Ministry of Transport, toward the end of 1947, for EMPIRE COPPICE, at the time under management. It was their intention that she be renamed ELKHOUND. The sale, however, was not concluded and she was sold to the Kuwait Oil Company.

Also during 1948 Hadley Shipping decided to re-enter the deep sea tanker market. The necessary Government Licence was obtained and they placed an order with the Greenock Dockyard Company for a new diesel powered vessel of around 16,500 tons deadweight for delivery in 1952. Whilst under construction she was fixed with a five year charter to the Anglo-Iranian Oil Company Ltd, later restyled as the British Petroleum Company Ltd. The Greenock Dockyard Company, a subsidiary of Cayzer, Irvine and Company (Clan Line), had lately been specializing in cargo-liner construction so the placing of this order and two by Norwegian owners marked a return to tanker

CERINTHUS (2) in Alexandra Dock, Liverpool   *(WSPL)*

31

building at the yard. The purchase price for the new vessel was £671,000 'subject to the customary increases in accordance with builders and engineers usual practice'. The time-charter rate was fixed at £1 per deadweight ton per month (£16,500). She was given the name CORATO after one of the original tankers in the fleet and was the first vessel to be bedecked with the new funnel markings of a black 'HSC' on a white diamond, superimposed on the original black topped yellow funnel. The house flag had been the black HSC on white diamond on a yellow field for some time. The new funnel markings were to cause some amusement within the Hadley/Houlder fleet. The HSC on the diamond were interpreted as Hadley's Sunshine Cruises or Houlder's Senior Company depending on one's point of view.

In 1950, The Hadley Shipping Company share distribution was:-

Walter Warwick	£52,000.
Immingham Agency Company Ltd	£36,000.
Coastal Tankers Ltd	£35,000.
National Bank and Sir John Esplen	£30,000.
Houlder Group of Companies	£23,000.
Cyril Warwick	£20,000.
Lady Aline O. Esplen	£19,000.
Executors of M.H. Warwick	£14,400.
Others	£70,600.
Total	£300,000.

During 1951 Coastal Tankers Ltd decided to quit the coastal tanker business, and accordingly sold OTTERHOUND to Canadian buyers. However they entered the dry cargo trade by purchasing GOLDDRIFT, GOLDEVE, GOLDFAUN, GOLDGNOME and GOLDHIND, all small coastal vessels, from E.J. and W. Goldsmith. Management of these vessels was, unusually, entrusted to the Springwell Shipping Company Ltd, with the exception of GOLDHIND which was initially managed by Immingham Agency, before being renamed PURPLE EMPEROR in 1952 and passing to Springwell management. Within months some of these vessels were sold or

CERINTHUS   (FotoFlite)

transferred to other family connected companies, such as Leadenhall Shipping Company.

CORATO was delivered on 21st March 1952. To assist with her financing it had been decided during 1951 to dispose of DAXHOUND to German buyers for £78,000. She eventually became the sludge carrier LUKI and had, at 58 years of age, a remarkably long life when disposed of to Italian shipbreakers in 1989. Also in 1951 came the outbreak of the Korean War which brought with it a considerable boom in the shipping world. Freight rates rose dramatically, as did ship values, and by early 1952 Hadley Shipping had decided to take advantage of the situation by selling the Liberty CERINTHUS. She was snapped up for £580,000 by Panamanian operators associated with the Greek Goulandris Group, returning a very satisfactory profit on her £135,000 purchase price. The funds realised from the sale of CERINTHUS enabled the company to embark on another deep sea tanker venture with Anglo-Saxon.

Shell's 'Sale & Charter Back'

The 1926 'Sale and Charter Back' programme remained in the memory at Shell, and was to be repeated. Post-1945 demand for oil grew and large orders were placed for ships, the backbone being the 18,000 dwt general purpose H/K class (British /Dutch flag), followed by their streamlined A-class sisters (total 86 units, including associated Eagle Oil Company ships). 1951/2 orders for 73 ships for delivery by the end of 1957 were followed by others including 34 placed in 1955.

The finance required for this programme led Shell to seek outside owners to take over contracts, finance, man and manage the ships under charter to Shell, in addition to finance houses involvement through Tanker Finance Ltd and Maatschappij Tot Financiering van Bedrijfspanden N.V. Cyril Warwick of Houlder Bros was asked by Shell to encourage British owners to take an interest in tankers and companies with which he was associated took part.

After their long association with Shell, Hadley Shipping were a natural partner and agreed to purchase a contract for an 'H' class, on order from Harland and Wolff Ltd, Belfast, for 1954 delivery and later that for an 'A' class to be completed in 1961 by Hawthorn, Leslie (Shipbuilders) Ltd, Hebburn.

Other ships similarly sold to shipowners and chartered back included (all H / K class unless stated - year of completion).
* A-class: ** R-class: + V-class: ++ Z-class.

EASTGATE (57)	STONEGATE (61)*	FORTHFIELD (55)
EDWARD STEVINSON (61)**	KAYESON (61)++	LLANISHEN (57)+
LLANGORSE (60)+	WILLIAM WHEELWRIGHT (60)**	
TINDFONN (61)**	DOELWIJK (63)++	VLIELAND (59)*
KAAP HOORN (58)	DORESTAD (55)	PURMEREND (57)
ALKMAAR (58)	SCHELPWIJK (55)	AMELAND (56)
MUNTTOREN (57)	WESTERTOREN (54)	

The 'H' class contract was the last of a trio, yard numbers 1468-HARPA, 1469-HARVELLA and 1470-un-named. No name had been allocated to 1470 at the time of purchase but shortly afterward Anglo-Saxon placed another order with Harland and Wolff for a sistership to be named HARPULA. One can only wonder if that had been the intended name for what became Hadley's CERINTHUS, delivered in 1954 to commence her time-charter to the Shell Tanker Company Ltd, as which the Anglo-Saxon Petroleum Company had recently been restyled. It was not possible in the conditions prevailing at the time to obtain a fixed price for the vessel but it was expected that it would be around £1,200,000. The contract was combined with an initial five year time-charter at the rate of £1 5s (£1.25p) per ton deadweight per month. It was, at that time, a matter of great satisfaction to the Company that they were able to renew their earlier association with Anglo-Saxon which had, as stated earlier, seen the formation of the Company in 1926. CERINTHUS had a very large and tall funnel. A Houlder Bros naval architect recalled James Huntly could not decide on the funnel, so he (the architect) made several cut-out funnels to scale and presented them to Huntly, who chose the largest.

In 1954 the remaining cargo vessels, managed by Springwell Shipping Company on behalf of the family companies, were transferred to Immingham Agency management. BASSETHOUND by this time was 20 years old and, although it had been hoped that her life could be prolonged by increasing her carrying capacity, this proved to be uneconomic and she was sold for £14,000. This ended the Company interest in coastal tanker operations.

During 1955 Esplen Trust Ltd purchased a small dry cargo coaster to fulfil a two year contract, trading between the Thames and the Seine in France. This vessel was, unusually, given the Hadley name CEPOLIS. Within months she had been transferred to Coastal Tankers' ownership, and for the duration of her contract, all three of the original Hadley names, CEPOLIS, CORATO and CERINTHUS, had been revived in the combined fleet.

In 1957, at the age of 70, James Huntly retired from all his directorships except Hadley Shipping, and settled in Bournemouth. He continued to take

CEPOLIS (2)   (WSPL)

an active interest in the Company until his death at the age of 90, in December 1977, only four days after attending a meeting in the Hadley offices. Lewis Warwick also decided to depart from Hadley Shipping around the same time and John Esplen was introduced by his father, Sir Graham Esplen, but with interests laying elsewhere he too departed from the Company within a few years.

This then left Hadley Shipping with a fleet of two deep-sea tankers, CORATO on charter to British Petroleum, and CERINTHUS chartered to Shell Tankers. CORATO was subsequently fixed with a charter to Caltex Petroleum Company. That was to be the situation for the next few years. However Shell Tankers had been continuing with their fleet modernisation programme and that in turn led to another offer to Hadley Shipping late in 1959. This time it was for a twenty year demise charter with an optional five year extension, for one of their A class 18,000 tons deadweight vessels already on order. It was combined with a new fifteen year demise charter, also with an optional five year extension for CERINTHUS, which had just completed her initial five year timecharter to Shell. In both cases these demise charters were coupled with a management agreement with Shell, whereby the Immingham Agency Company would manage both ships on behalf of Shell for an agreed fee. This was unusual for a demise or bareboat charter, as charterers normally manage the ship themselves. It was felt that this was an ideal arrangement for both Hadley and Immingham. It would safeguard the future of both companies and, at the same time, would leave CORATO free to take advantage of any improvement in the market. Shell incidentally made similar arrangements with several other British owners, amongst them Turnbull Scott and Company, Ropner Shipping Company and Evan Thomas Radcliffe.

CLYMENE, as the new ship was named, was launched by Miss Elizabeth Rowell, daughter of the Chairman of Hawthorn Leslie, where the ship was built, and the name was chosen by the sponsor. CLYMENE was the first vessel in the world to have epoxy coated tanks and upon completion in 1961 entered onto the 20 year charter with Shell.

Whereas CERINTHUS, being a black oil ship, traded much of her life in the Atlantic, along the east coast of South America, the Caribbean and U.S. Atlantic Seaboard including the occasional voyage to Manaos, a thousand miles up the Amazon, CLYMENE was under the direction of Shell Eastern, based in Singapore, and traded mainly in the Far East, Australia, New Zealand and the Pacific. As a clean oil tanker with coated tanks, she was chartered by Shell to the Americans during the Vietnam War and made numerous trips with aviation spirit for the U.S. Air Force. When proceeding up river to the fuel dump she was always escorted by a fleet of gunboats as protection against any Viet Cong guerillas who might be lurking in the undergrowth. The entire crew were, of course, paid a Vietnam bonus of 100% for a minimum of five days even if they were only in Vietnam waters for a day. For this reason a posting to the vessel was a popular assignment as she never encountered any problems.

CLYMENE (1)

Fred's lot.

CERINTHUS and CLYMENE, both standard Shell designs and chartered to that company, had one major difference, recalled Fred Lott who served as Chief Engineer on both. Joining CLYMENE as 2nd engineer in 1961 (promoted to Chief the following year) he found a very reliable set of machinery - as he wrote '. . . virtually the engine room ran itself'. Transferring to CERINTHUS in 1965 he found machinery which would present problems when least expected. On one occasion she was proceeding down river after discharging at the Shell refinery near Rouen, when an electric cable failure caused complete machinery stoppage. CERINTHUS had to be towed out of the river to an anchorage where the engine room crew proceeded to repair the damage. She was very well known to ship repairers at Cardiff, Barry and Swansea! A notable character on CERINTHUS was 'Jimmy', the Chinese laundry man. When boiler cleaning took place he was always in the engine room doing his share, and was known to instruct the Chief Engineer to put on an old boiler suit or else he would refuse to wash it.

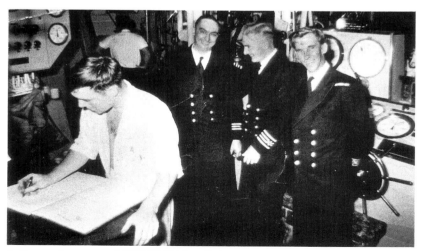

In the engine room of CLYMENE (1) at Nelson, New Zealand. (Left to right) Captain W.S.S. Lewis, Chief Engineer C.H. Wall and Fred Lott. In foreground Junior Engineer A. Lowry

TURMOIL and FLYING ENTERPRISE

In 1941 James Huntly had become a director of the Overseas Towage and Salvage Company Ltd, a company formed a few years previously, with a base in Milford Haven, as Britain's re-entry into the deep-sea towage industry (United Towing Ltd, Hull, had been undertaking deep-sea towing work for many years prior to this time, but had not touched the salvage aspect with purpose built deep-sea tugs). Three tugs were ordered:-

NEPTUNIA	1938	798g.	sunk by U 29 on 13th September 1939.
SALVONIA	1939	571g.	sold 1947, renamed ABEILLE No.25.
NEREIDIA	1939	327g.	sold 1939, renamed ABEILLE No.4.

A large fleet of tugs was also managed for the Ministry of War Transport during World War II.

Undoubtedly the most famous member of the fleet was the motor tug TURMOIL (1,136g./45), chartered from the Admiralty between 1948 and 1963 (she was broken up in 1986 as the Greek MATSAS). During this period she was manned, like Hadley Shipping, from the Houlder pool.

TURMOIL 'hit the headlines' in the early days of 1952. On 21st December 1951 FLYING ENTERPRISE (6,711g./44) had sailed from Hamburg for New York. On 28th December in a force 12 hurricane her cargo shifted and a split developed in her hull in 49.20N 17.20W. Distress signals were answered by SHERBOURNE, SOUTHLAND, NOORDAM, GENERAL A.W. GREELY and WAR HAWK. The following day passengers and crew were taken off by SOUTHLAND and GENERAL A.W. GREELY, leaving Captain Kurt Carlsen to await the arrival of a tug.

The salvage tugs were busy. OCEAAN set out for FLYING ENTERPRISE, but diverted to assist ZWARTE ZEE being driven onto a lee shore with her tow. TURMOIL was committed to the tanker MACTRA which had lost it's propeller. Having completed the MACTRA service, TURMOIL proceeded to FLYING ENTERPRISE on 2nd January. Efforts to connect the tow were foiled by continued bad weather. Two days later Kenneth Dancy, a Hadley officer on relief duties as mate of TURMOIL, managed to join Carlsen on the casualty and they connected the line. Towing conditions were abysmal, the damage to FLYING ENTERPRISE and bad weather limited the speed possible as TURMOIL made for Falmouth. By the afternoon of 10th January the funnel of FLYING ENTERPRISE was slapping the water. There was no chance now of saving her, Carlsen and Dancy jumped into the sea and were picked up by TURMOIL. Less than an hour later FLYING ENTERPRISE sank, 60 miles from Falmouth in 49.38N 4.23W, some 670 miles from where TURMOIL had picked her up.

Soon after TURMOIL went to assist another casualty drifting with her propeller lost in bad weather. A connection was made with the Liberty ship ROBERT H. HARRISON and after a week fighting the elements she was brought into Liverpool.

Thompson, saw modifications to the Greek ships in the light of Hadley's experience, particularly in respect of the ballast hold.

Since the outset there had always been strong links between Hadley Shipping and Houlder Bros. The latter still held their original shareholding in the Company, supplying all Hadley's crews, and both Walter and Cyril Warwick had served on Houlder's Board, whilst John Houlder had joined the Hadley Board in 1947. Following discussions with Houlder Brothers and their subsidiary Empire Transport Company it was decided that ownership of the new vessel would be shared equally between Hadley and the two Houlder companies, although she would operate in the Hadley fleet under Warwick and Esplen's management. All three of the partners obtained an investment grant from the British Government.

Captain Trevor White, as owner's Superintendent, was sent to stand by CLYDESDALE at the builders yard and thanks to his eagle eye what otherwise could have been an embarrassing situation was averted just before she commenced her sea-trials. He became aware that the position of the hawse pipe was such that when the anchor was dropped it would go straight through the bulbous bow. When approached, the builders insisted it was not the case, so a demonstration was arranged which proved Captain White's case. Rather than redesign the bows, a large notice was hung in the wheelhouse to the effect that prior to anchoring the anchor should be walked out until clear of the bow. CLYDESDALE was completed in October 1967, at a cost of almost £2million, and for the first year or so of her life was employed tramping on the open market, often with cargoes of grain from the U.S. Gulf to Rotterdam.

Late in 1965 a number of leading British shipowners had formed a consortium to build and operate a fleet of large bulk carriers, against which they would secure contract business, the hope being that their operating philosophy would lead to their becoming a dominant force in the market. The owners involved were Bibby Line, Shipping and Industrial Holdings (parent company of H. Clarkson and Company, the leading shipbrokers), Silver Line and Britain Steamship Company (Watts, Watts and Company). Named Seabridge Shipping Ltd., they were later joined by the Bowring S.S. Company Ltd, and Hunting and Son.

The arrangement was that all vessels built by the participants were in effect timechartered to Seabridge, who were the commercial operators of the fleet, from their own office. The daily rate of hire paid by Seabridge to the Owners for each vessel was assessed by means of a complicated points system which took into account the differing characteristics of each vessel.

In 1968 Houlder Brothers and their parent Furness, Withy and Company decided to join the Seabridge consortium and their bulk carriers were accordingly entered into Seabridge. It was a rule that no member, for obvious reasons, was permitted to operate any bulk carrier on the market in competition with Seabridge. This in practice meant any vessel over 35,000 tons deadweight. Therefore, because of Houlder's shared ownership with Hadley of the CLYDESDALE, she too had to be entered into Seabridge, being renamed CLYDE BRIDGE to conform with their naming policy. Hadley, in effect if not in name, became members of Seabridge.

Like so many things, it seemed a good thing at the time, but in the end proved to be a very unfortunate decision not only for Houlders but also for Hadley. Seabridge certainly enabled the participating members to build up a large fleet, as a timecharter to Seabridge, which in essence was effectively to themselves, enabled the participants to raise the necessary bank finance (banks were a little more gullible in those days, the years following World War I being long forgotten), and at one stage a fleet of over 2 million tons deadweight was being operated. However, not only were the trading results most disappointing, but another rule of the Seabridge pool, requiring three years notice to withdraw a ship, had the effect of preventing members from taking advantage of a firm market and selling vessels when markets were high, thus enabling them to reinvest at a later stage when markets were weaker, an essential feature of successful tramp shipowning. Furthermore a firm market paradoxically meant that Seabridge, if anything, was turning in poorer results because that was when charterers exercised options to ship even more cargo under contracts, many of which were at best showing only relatively modest returns to Seabridge. This in turn meant Seabridge had insufficient tonnage and had to charter in vessels at high market rates to cover additional cargo being shipped under the options. This, combined with late deliveries of newbuildings, compounded an already bad situation. The continuing disappointing results finally caused the participants to rethink their strategy, with the result they steadily cut back their involvement, until eventual withdrawal. By 1980 Seabridge was left with one participant, Silver Line. Silver Line, since 1974, had been a member of the Vlassov Group, who retained Seabridge as a contract and marketing member of the Group.

So, all in all, Seabridge proved to be a very disappointing exercise for it's members. It is of course true that, without Seabridge, the majority of it's members would never have engaged in operating bulk carriers on such a large scale, but it is equally true to say that this was at considerable cost. The ships earned very poor returns and the fact that owners could not sell at the right time made matters worse. If anything membership of Seabridge probably played a part in accelerating the final withdrawal from shipowning of some of it's members.

As part of a planned expansion programme, and at a cost of around £280,000 each, Hadley Shipping ordered three vessels of the short sea trading type from the Dutch NESCOS Group, all three obtaining an investment grant. The first of the trio was delivered as CAMARINA during 1969, followed closely by CORATO. They were innovative inasmuch as their main engine was controlled from the bridge.

Shortly after they entered service Cyril Warwick, at the age of 69, retired from Chairmanship of Houlder Brothers in December 1969. He also retired from his numerous Board appointments within the Furness Withy Group, to concentrate his interests as Chairman of Hadley Shipping.

Launch of CAMARINA. Note protection of houses on opposite bank
(Fotobureau Folkers)

In 1969 the Alexander Shipping Company, a Houlder subsidiary, was building a 15,000 ton tweendecker, with substantial container capacity, at Scott's Shipbuilding and Engineering Company, Greenock, when the yard approached them to ask if they would be interested in taking over a contract for a bulk carrier which had been ordered by Greek interests.   Scotts' indicated that a quick decision was necessary.   Neither Alexander nor Houlders were interested, so Hadley were approached. The upshot was, that

by the evening of the same day, Hadley had taken over a contract for a 31,000 ton bulk carrier fitted with two twelve ton derricks at each of her seven hatches, for delivery in 1971 at a price of £2 million. The company obtained a loan of 70% from the Shipbuilding Industries Board. Although CYMBELINE was considered, the name CUMBRIA was chosen for the new ship which was launched on 14th May 1971 by Iona Warwick, the daughter of Peter Warwick. At the age of seven she was reported to have been the

P.J. Warwick, appointed Chairman in 1985
(Publifoto)

youngest sponsor ever to launch a ship on the lower reaches of the Clyde. CUMBRIA was delivered from her builders on 1st July 1971, when she entered into a two year time-charter to Japan Line which was subsequently extended for a further two years. The first two years trading was mainly with ore from India to Japan and then the vessel was fixed back to the Atlantic. Whilst performing a voyage from Oxelosund in Sweden to Emden with an ore cargo in September 1973 she ran aground on the island of Samso in the Great Belt (Denmark) during bad weather. At the subsequent Inquiry it was discovered that a number of charts on the vessel, although marked as corrected had, in fact, not been corrected and one of these charts, which did not show the altered position of a buoy marking a sandbank, was being used for navigation when the vessel grounded.

The vessel made strenuous efforts to refloat under her own power by going astern, to no avail and it was only when going ahead was tried, that she slid over the sandbank into deep water. She suffered severe bottom damage, but managed to reach Emden where she discharged and was then drydocked at Antwerp for repairs.

Meanwhile, a new Manager was appointed to the Company in 1969. Peter Kittermaster had been previously employed by Christian Salvesen of Leith and he set about reforming the structure of the Company. In 1970 the co-operation enjoyed with Houlder Brothers, whereby the latter's Technical Department supervised the building and running of Hadley ships, was terminated in a cost cutting operation. John M. Reid, formerly of Clan Line and the Greek Niarchos Group, was appointed Chief Superintendent and henceforth assumed responsibility for the activities previously cared for by Houlder staff. However the transfer of sea staff between Furness / Houlder and Hadley continued unchanged until 1986 when the technical management and crewing of Hadley vessels was transferred to the Everard and Denholm ship management operations. At this juncture the Technical Department was shut down. Commercial management, apart from that of COTINGA with Everard, was retained by Warwick and Esplen Ltd.

The last of the Dutch trio arrived from the shipyard as CALANDRIA in 1970. Shortly after the 1971 delivery of CUMBRIA, Sir Graham Esplen, one of the original Directors of the Company, retired.

CALANDRIA in the Clyde, passing CUMBRIA fitting out

Nescos.

On 29th October 1937, Nescos Scheepsbouwcombinatie B.V. (Nescos Shipbuilding Association Ltd), Groningen, was formed by shipbuilders in the Province of Groningen to promote the sale and export of ships constructed in their yards. In the 1960s like other combines such as Conoship, Nescos provided central design, marketing and supply services for the yards.

A range of standard designs was marketed, the building of which could be undertaken by any member yard. Orders were allocated to the yard with capacity available to give the earliest delivery, or best suited to meet buyers needs. They were:-

Bodewes' Scheepswerven B.V., Hoogezand.
B.V. v/h Scheepswerven Gebr. van Diepen, Waterhuizen.
Scheepsbouw -en - Reparatiebedrijf Gebr. Sander B.V., Delfzijl.
E.J. Smit & Zoon's Scheepswerven B.V., Westerbroek.
Scheepswerf Gebr. Suurmeijer B.V., Foxhol.

Gebr. Suurmeijer went bankrupt in 1979. Gebr. Sander resigned from Nescos in July 1979 with plans to join the Conoship Group, but instead amalgamated with Scheepswerf Appingedam-Niestern, Delfzijl, in November 1980 as Niestern-Sander B.V.

The remaining three yards split up about 1986. E.J. Smit & Zoon became bankrupt in July 1987, one of the oldest yards in the Province of Groningen, since when the sole partner in NESCOS has been the Bodewes shipyard at Martenshoek.

In collaboration with the Danish shipowner Rederiet Otto Danielsen, NESCOS identified a gap for a standard design in the newbuilding market, a design which could be developed into a range of sizes and be fitted out to meet owners needs. Otto Danielsen offered their services to manage any of the vessels ordered by owners.

One variation was the 1600 / 2650 dwt open / closed shelter decker. Twelve ships of this design were built by NESCOS member yards for U.K. based owners. Apart from Hadley's three, other examples went to Hall Brothers S.S. Company Ltd, Newcastle (2), Turnbull, Scott and Company Ltd, Farnborough (2), Park Steamships Ltd (a Danielsen subsidiary in partnership with John Denham a director of H. Clarkson and Company, and W.J.P. "Chile" Chambers of the Liverpool shipowning family), London (2), Harrisons (Clyde) Ltd, Glasgow (2) and Shaw, Savill and Albion Company Ltd, London (1).

The Esplen family, who had been involved with the Company since the early days, decided to dispose of their assets during 1973. John Esplen, the son of Sir Graham Esplen, had retired in 1971, resigning his seat on the Board. Some 75,000 shares, representing 10% of the share capital, were then sold to the Denholm Line of Steamers, the balance being purchased by Warwick and Esplen Ltd. J.D.D. Brown, a member of the Denholm Family, was invited to join the Board.

In 1972 Houlder Brothers acquired the management of the Wm France Fenwick fleet, at that time owned by Jessel Securities. There were four ships under Houlder management, STAR PINEWOOD, an open hatch bulk carrier fitted with gantry cranes and operating in the Norwegian STAR pool, and three colliers SHERWOOD, CHELWOOD and DALEWOOD. Of these three SHERWOOD was operating on the charter market, CHELWOOD was on a long term charter to the Central Electricity Generating Board, whilst DALEWOOD was coming to the end of a similar long term charter. STAR PINEWOOD was subsequently sold to Stamford Shipping Company, a Fred Olsen Company, and renamed STAR BULFORD.

One morning in March 1974 Jessel Securities telephoned Houlder Brothers to tell them that they wished to sell their remaining three ships, but the sale had to be concluded the very same day, a tall order indeed. In these circumstances Houlder Brothers, who, by virtue of the fact that they were managing the three ships and so knew all about them, were the obvious buyers. They did not have to inspect the ships to assess their condition and in the time available it was impossible for anyone else to do so. Unfortunately, however, the necessary Furness Withy authority for the whole deal was unavailable in the time scale required, and so it was agreed that Hadley, who were interested in acquiring one or more of the vessels, would acquire all three, giving Houlders the option of purchasing, on the same terms, SHERWOOD plus either CHELWOOD or DALEWOOD, at Houlder's choice. Houlders quickly exercised their option of purchasing SHERWOOD, but found it difficult to choose between CHELWOOD and DALEWOOD. Outwardly they were similar but internally there was one major difference, the engine. CHELWOOD had a one-off Werkspoor engine, the only one of it's type ever built, spares were expensive and difficult to come by and, consequently, her operating costs were much higher than DALEWOOD which had a 3,800 bhp Sulzer, built in Switzerland, which ran like a sewing machine and never gave any trouble. On the other hand CHELWOOD had the security of a seven year charter to the Central Electricity Generating Board, whereas the charter of DALEWOOD, to the

OSWESTRY GRANGE in the Tyne   (W.J. Harvey)

same organization, was just about to finish and market prospects were looking uncertain. So, Houlders plumped for CHELWOOD which was renamed OSWESTRY GRANGE, leaving Hadley with DALEWOOD for which they paid £850,000, being the only vessel which became registered to them from the transaction. In the end there was satisfaction all round, because DALEWOOD's charter to the Central Electricity Generating Board was in fact extended for a further seven years and, if anything, Hadley probably came out better than Houlder, because DALEWOOD, which was later renamed CYMBELINE had the lower operating costs.

But, also in 1974 following their purchase of DALEWOOD, and with the deepsea market looking a little shaky, Hadley decided it would be prudent to dispose of their half share in CLYDE BRIDGE to Houlders, who had a tax driven investment requirement. And so she passed to Houlders yielding a profit on sale to Hadley of some £1.9 million. But, as part of the deal, Hadley agreed to charter her back, under Warwick and Esplen management until early 1977, at a rate which showed a loss to Hadley of about £180,000 per annum. By then Houlders had withdrawn from the illfated Seabridge Consortium and, on conclusion of her charter to Hadley, her management was handed over to Houlders and she was renamed DUNSTER GRANGE.

Although the earnings of CLYDE BRIDGE had been very disappointing, operationally she had run very well apart from two incidents, the first of which occurred in the St Lawrence River. Late in 1971, the vessel had loaded a cargo of sugar in Durban, at 34,157 tons the largest cargo so far shipped from that port, which was destined for Montreal. On her previous passage, an ore cargo from Canada to Italy, the vessel was severely delayed discharging in Italy (taking nearly a month instead of a few days). The result being, that by the time she arrived at the mouth of the St Lawrence, after loading in South Africa, it was very late in the season and ice had begun to form in the river. She then suffered further delay due to a St Lawrence River Pilot strike. When she eventually proceeded to Montreal it was suddenly noticed that she was going down by the head and taking water. She put into Quebec where severe bottom damage was discovered. Half the cargo was lightened at Quebec, being shipped by rail to Montreal in the Spring. This enabled the vessel to proceed to Montreal to discharge the balance in mid-February 1972. By this time winter had well and truly set in and considerable difficulty was experienced in discharging the cargo and the service of the local fire brigade had to be called upon to pump ballast because the ballast lines had frozen. When CLYDE BRIDGE eventually sailed from Montreal on 18th January she was able to follow a Manchester Liners vessel which created a passage through the ice. She eventually reached Baltimore without incident, where the damage to the bottom was repaired. It was fortunate that the winter was not particularly severe that year because the vessel, although not ice classed, suffered no ice damage at all apart from scratched paint. It was never conclusively explained what caused the bottom damage in the first place, but the vessel had obviously hit some form of underwater obstruction. One theory was she had struck a large submerged tree trunk, the end of which was embedded in the bottom of the river. Suffice to say, however, the whole episode resulted in a major legal battle mainly over who was responsible for the damage to the sugar whilst it was lying at Quebec. The legal arguments went on for years and when Hadley's lawyers eventually wrote to say that the case had been finally settled they made the comment "it is like saying goodbye to an old friend".

The other earlier incident which befell CLYDE BRIDGE was during the middle of a Transpacific passage with coal, from Norfolk for Japan. She sailed from Norfolk on 6th May 1970 and suffered an explosion on 22nd May which blew the No.4 hatchcover off. The reason for this was never satisfactorily explained, but it was felt the most likely theory was that a flint had become embedded in the hatch rubber and the working of the ship had caused a spark as the flint came into contact with the steel of the hatch cover, resulting in an explosion in the gas produced by the cargo. Putting into Honolulu two days after the explosion, CLYDE BRIDGE was unable to replace the $7\frac{1}{2}$ ton hatch cover as she had no cargo gear. A floating crane had to be hired, and the damaged hatch was lashed down and covered in tarpaulins until repairs could be carried out at Sasebo, Japan.

The remaining capital from the sale of CLYDE BRIDGE was invested in a new vessel for 1976 delivery. This time it was for a gearless mini bulk carrier, to another Dutch NESCOS design which was finding favour with several British operators but in fewer numbers than the earlier design. Turnbull, Scott Ltd ordered two, Park Steamship Company Ltd and Hadley Shipping Company Ltd one each. As the Denholm family had become shareholders in Hadley it came as no surprise that they ordered three units for their own shipping operation as GALLIC WAVE, MARY ANDERSON and

MISHNISH, all three being initially operated within the Norwegian controlled A/S Kristian Jebsens bulk carrier pool.

The original Dutch (Park class) trio, CAMARINA and her sisters, all included liner charters in their careers. The Gracechurch Line, operated to Libya by Newcastle based Anthony and Bainbridge and Witherington and Everett, had several similar ships on charter from other owners when, in 1974 / 75, they suddenly found themselves shipless with cargo waiting to be loaded. The Spanish built (super Park class) WAYNEGATE had lost her rudder in the Bay of Biscay on 13th November 1974 and was towed into El Ferrol. Consequent on this her two sisterships NARYA and NENYA were drydocked at Taranto and on the Tyne in January and February 1975. Both had to have their rudder stocks renewed. CALANDRIA was available and chartered to help fill this gap and a happy relationship developed which saw all three Hadley sisters employed on the Gracechurch Line for a number of years -

CALANDRIA	14.4.1975 to 26. 5.1979
CORATO	14.3.1977 to 2. 7.1978
CAMARINA	14.3.1978 to 19.12.1979

When 1975 eventually arrived it brought a mixed bag of fortunes for the Company. The most severe blow was the termination of the Shell time charters. This had come about when Shell made an approach to the Company requesting that consideration be given to the possibility of the premature termination of the two charter arrangements. CERINTHUS was by this time

CORATO (3) at Malta on charter to Gracechurch Line   *(WSPL)*

22 years old and her charter had just under four years to run whilst CLYMENE at fifteen years of age had five years to run. Both vessels, having steam turbine propulsion, were by now proving much too costly to run, due to relatively high fuel consumption, a feature of the turbine, coupled with a very depressed tanker market. It was these factors which caused Shell to seek the ending of their charters. A suitable agreement was thrashed out

whereby Shell would compensate Hadley, and in 1976 both ships were sold for scrap. CERINTHUS completed her last voyage from Swansea to Stanlow before proceeding to Faslane, and CLYMENE from Australia to Singapore thence to her end in Taiwan. With their departure came the final withdrawal from the tanker trades. It is to be remembered that Shell under it's old guise of Anglo-Saxon created the opportunity to enter the tanker business and also took the Company out of it 50 years later. The Company received £1,450,000 compensation from Shell for loss of earnings based on the remaining charter periods, coupled with sundry payments which would have been made to Hadley had the charters continued.

Shell's 'Tanker Economy Drive'

In 1975 Shell undertook a radical look at their tanker operations and as a result embarked on a cost-cutting operation. Apart from terminating charter contracts like those with Hadley Shipping for their two old turbine tankers they also looked at their own fleet and implemented a variation of their two earlier sale and charterback agreements. In 1976, six M-class (built 1968-70, c105,000g.) VLCC's (Very Large Crude Carriers) were sold to Greek and Norwegian owners. The contracts included charters for tankers with more economical machinery than the turbines of the M-class. Goulandris (United Shipping and Trading Company of Greece S.A.) took MEGARA, MANGELIA and MELANIA with charters for ANDROS ATLAS and ANDROS ARIES (both 119,505g./72) and ANDROS CHRYSSI (129,795g./74). Niarchos purchased MELO and chartered ATHINA S. NIARCHOS (106,623g./72) whilst Sig Bergesen exchanged MYSELLA and MARTICIA for BERGE SEPTIMUS (139,780g./74) and BERGE DUKE (139,776g./73).

Peter Warwick was on board CERINTHUS during her last working voyage and stated that although she was a hard working ship, with very poor accommodation, he was moved by the affection shown for the 'old lady' and noted the real air of sadness and nostalgia amongst the crew when they walked down the gangway for the last time. He was also able to visit CLYMENE just before her demise and recalled that just prior to her unexpected sale the vessel had done a six month stay in Australia and had a large quantity of prime Australian beef on board. Whilst the vessel was lying in Singapore before going to the breakers in Taiwan, arrangements were made to give away the surplus stock of meat to an orphanage run by nuns in Singapore, but at the last minute the customs refused to give permission for the meat to be sent ashore. So instructions were sent to the Chief Steward that the entire crew were to be fed prime steak morning, noon and night. "I happened to be in Singapore at the time and was rather surprised to be offered a Cornish Pasty for lunch when I went on board" he recalled. It seemed that the Chief Steward, faithful to his profession to the last, was hanging on to the stores to the bitter end and just could not bring himself to distribute such largesse.

It was a very sad day for the Company when their long standing relationship with Shell, which spanned a half century, finally came to an end. There was a brief reunion however when, on 4th October 1977, Shell hosted a celebration dinner party at Shell Centre in London to mark the 50th anniversary of the original "Sale and Charter Back". Representatives of the shipping companies who participated in the original deals were invited. With the exception of Cyril Warwick representing Hadley and Fred Newman of Davies and Newman all the other guests were Norwegian.

On the happier side COTINGA was launched on the 10th September 1976 by Miss Belinda Hood, a grand-daughter of Company Chairman Cyril Warwick. This event was something of an event to witness. The locality of the shipyard on the Martenshoek-Foxhol Canal necessitates a sideways launch into the canal. However, such is the effect of a launch that it is necessary to take precautions on the opposite bank. The villa overlooking the launch site has to have it's windows and doors boarded up to withstand the battering incurred by the resultant wave of muddy water and pebbles.

Revenue from the tanker disposals coupled with satisfactory earnings in the dry cargo market prompted the planning of further ships. With COTINGA completing in Holland, it was decided that another vessel of similar size be ordered for 1978 delivery. Once again the Denholm connection was to feature. This mini-bulk carrier, ordered during 1977 from Appledore Shipbuilders, was to a similar design as Denholms GALLIC FJORD, MARKINCH and LESLIE GAULT, but would differ in that she would be fitted with three five ton Sherwen electro-hydraulic cranes. She

LESLIE GAULT in the Elbe   (W.J. Harvey)

was allocated the name CERINTHUS and was completed at a fixed cost of £1,632,000.

A year later the opportunity arose of a time-charter to the Canadian newsprint producer Consolidated Bathurst, who were looking for a suitable vessel to carry newsprint from their plant at Port Alfred on the Saguenay River, a tributary of the St Lawrence, to Purfleet on the Thames and Ellesmere Port on the Manchester Ship Canal. Newsprint, which is shipped in large rolls, is a very delicate cargo requiring careful handling and calls for a specialized type of vessel, at that time with large and clear box type holds and hatches extending the full width of the holds. Furthermore, as both the St Lawrence and Saguenay River freeze in winter, a vessel of high ice class is essential. It so happened that a French liner company, Compagnie de Navale Chargeurs Delmas-Vieljeux (S.N.C.D.V.), had two very suitable vessels for sale, BARBIZON and her sister BOCHICA (launched as

JODEW). BARBIZON had a very chequered history. Originally built for Norwegian owners as JOCARE, she was part of a six ship order in 1975 at the VEB Schiffswerft "Neptun" yard in Rostock in East Germany. She was of the so-called 'Rostock' design 8,000 tons deadweight single decker with two large box type holds, suitable for containers, each served by two 22 ton swinging derricks, and of highest ice class. Shortly after delivery the Norwegian owners got into financial difficulties and the vessel was sold to the French Compagnie de Nav. Mixte, but they kept her for only one year as OYAPOK before passing her on to Delmas-Vieljeux who employed her again for only one year on their Mediterannean container trade as BARBIZON, before offering her for sale. The fact that the vessel had had three owners in as many years was a matter for concern to Hadley but an exhaustive inspection could find nothing wrong with her and so she was purchased in June 1979 for just over £2 million and renamed CLYMENE for her time charter to Consolidated Bathurst, which was eventually to last five years. During her period of charter CLYMENE wore the funnel colours of her charterers as opposed to the Hadley HSC insignia.

All in all CLYMENE, which was a relatively small ship for the rigours of the North Atlantic especially in winter, performed forty eight transatlantic voyages, the outward voyages mainly in ballast, without incident apart from one occasion when a frozen pipe burst causing considerable damage to the newsprint in No.1 hold. But by the end of her charter the newsprint trade had moved on and a new breed of vessel was coming into vogue, with side ports enabling cargo to be loaded through the side of the ship. This was a considerable advantage inasmuch as it in effect enabled the cargo to be loaded during rain or snow, whereas in the more traditional type of vessel, such as CLYMENE, the hatches had to be closed immediately bad weather threatened, to prevent the newsprint getting wet. So at the end of the charter Consolidated Bathurst announced they had no further use for the vessel and alternative employment had to be found for her. The Company was fortunate to find this with the Central Electricity Generating Board alongside CYMBELINE, in the coastal coal trade between Newcastle and Sunderland to the Thames and Medway, for which her derricks were removed to facilitate cargo handling. Altogether CLYMENE was on charter to the Electricity Board for two years, spanning the miners strike, during which the vessel lay idle for several months on the Tyne thereafter performing several voyages to the Baltic before returning to the coal trade when the strike was over.

To help finance the purchase of BARBIZON, CORATO was sold in October 1978, followed by CALANDRIA in August 1979, the price achieved for the two vessels totalling only £518,454, whilst the last of the Dutch trio, CAMARINA, was sold two years later. The reason for the disposal of the trio was a combination of age, speed and the fact that they were rapidly becoming outmoded for market requirements.

CONTRACTION and CONSOLIDATION   *8*

The early part of 1979 saw the dry cargo market beginning to recover from the slump that had been brought about in 1974 primarily by the very large increase in oil prices, and by the end of 1980 reached it's peak as a result of large coal movements together with substantial grain imports by the U.S.S.R. At this time CUMBRIA was on time-charter to Russian operators and in December 1980, the Company received an approach from them, offering to purchase her outright. Lengthy negotiations ensued and the vessel was eventually sold for $12,990,000.   The Company was insisting on $13 million, but the Russians professed superstition resulting in the reduction in price of $10,000, with the vessel being delivered during February 1981. This sale, as it happened, coincided with the peak of the market after which the effects of the flood of newbuildings ordered during the boom of 1979/80 began to be felt. With this the market began to fall away and the period between 1981 and 1986 was one of severe depression, as bad if not worse than that of the 1930s, with many famous shipping companies sinking without a trace.

Only two years later, in 1983, a contract was purchased for a bulk carrier which was building at Varna, in Bulgaria, for Russian interests.   The

COTINGA and CELTIC ENDEAVOUR laid up at Newport Docks, 30 September 1983
(N.J. Cutts)

nameless ship was completed as CORATO, under Bermuda registry. After a maiden voyage via the Great Lakes with steel out and grain home, the vessel was chartered by the British Government for a project in the Falkland Islands following their recapture by British forces. Following conversion work at Swansea, which included the removal of her forward crane and the construction of a helicopter deck over the forward two hatches, she sailed on the 4th November 1983 for Port Stanley where she embarked a party of Royal Engineers, thereafter sailing to a remote bay in the Western part of the Falkland Islands where she lay at a mooring buoy for some five months. The purpose of the exercise was the construction of a radar site with associated buildings. For the duration of her stay the Royal Engineer lived on board CORATO which had brought all the necessary construction materials with her from Swansea. Every morning they flew off to progress the construction work ashore, returning in the evening. The fact that CORATO had accommodation for fifty three on board (standard Easter Bloc practice at the time), whereas Hadley operated her with only twenty three crew, was of great assistance in accommodating the party of Royal Engineers, and was one of the factors which led to the ship being chartered for the project in the first place. Throughout the period CORATO was completely independent of shore assistance, with the crew doing much of the cargo work and operating ship cranes, although the Royal Air Force did occasionally fly the crew to Port Stanley in the helicopter for a night on the town. In all the charter to the Ministry of Defence lasted some eight months and quite apart from having had the satisfaction of being able to play a part in the Falklands campaign, or at least it's aftermath, the Company was very pleased to have had the business at a time when freight markets had all but collapsed.

In 1984, both CORATO and CYMBELINE were redelivered from their respective charters, CYMBELINE being sold. Upon Cyril Warwick's retirement at the age of 85, in March 1985, he was succeeded as Chairman by Peter Warwick, a great-nephew of Walter Warwick. Unfortunately he was not to enjoy a lengthy retirement, as he died on the 14th July, barely four months later. The Company at this time was in a strong financial position following the sale of CUMBRIA and CYMBELINE, but nevertheless it was felt prudent to dispose of both CLYMENE, following the expiration of the C.E.G.B. contract, and CERINTHUS during 1986. This, once again, returned the Company to a fleet of only two vessels, COTINGA and CORATO. COTINGA had been in short term lay-up but subsequently returned to trade under the commercial management of F.T. Everard and Sons Ltd, London.

In September 1985 CORATO was chartered by the Ministry of Defence for a N.A.T.O. convoy exercise from Lisbon to Torbay. Although she had to ballast from Porsgrunn in Norway and wait for seven days before being delivered to the Ministry of Defence, the rate paid for the charter was sufficient to enable Hadley to absorb these costs. It was a 14 knot convoy, and CORATO was particularly attractive to her charterers because her 12,000 bhp engine gave ample reserve speed. She could operate at 16 knots,

although she never did so in Hadley service because the increased fuel consumption made it uneconomic. At her normal 14 knot service speed she burned 28 tons of fuel a day. In addition her numerous spare cabins were very useful, as they had been earlier in the Falklands, enabling her to accommodate the Portuguese naval officer who acted as convoy commodore, along with his staff. CORATO was reported sunk twice on the run from Lisbon to Torbay by a participating submarine.

1986 saw the market at it's lowest ebb with a large number of ships going to the breakers yards and very few new ships on order. The Company felt that there was scope for improvement in the market. Accordingly in October steps were taken to acquire another ship. QUEEN NORA, a Panamax type bulk carrier, was purchased for $5.5 million from Citibank, her mortgagees. She became the third CLYMENE and the largest ship to be owned by the Company. She was subsequently to take the Company into a war zone for the third time in recent years, but on this occasion it was not to their advantage. In January 1991 CLYMENE was on passage from Houston to Aqaba in Jordan with a cargo of wheat. Just before the vessel arrived at the Suez Canal, United Nations forces launched their offensive against Iraq, which by this time was already subject to U.N. sanctions. When CLYMENE arrived at the Straits of Tiran at the entrance to the Gulf of Aqaba she was intercepted by a patrolling U.S. warship, SAMUEL S. ROBERTS, which was part of the U.N. interdiction force enforcing U.N. sanctions. CLYMENE was ordered to stop and the SAMUEL S. ROBERTS sent a heavily armed boarding party. The entire crew was lined up on deck at gunpoint, whilst the boarding party proceeded to search the ship. In spite of the fact that her cargo had been shipped under a U.S. Aid programme to Jordan, the Commander of the American warship was not satisfied that the cargo was actually for consumption within Jordan, he considered it was going to be trans-shipped through Jordan to Iraq. CLYMENE was refused permission to proceed to Aqaba and told to take the cargo somewhere else! Several days of frantic activity ensued in Hadley's office whilst efforts were made to resolve the situation. The assistance of the U.S. State Department, the British Foreign Office, Ministry of Defence, the U.S. and British Ambassadors in Amman and the American Commander of the U.N. interdiction force in Bahrein under whose authority the SAMUEL S. ROBERTS was operating, were all enlisted but to no avail. They all took the view that it was someone elses problem and that the warship Commander, as the man on the spot, had complete authority to do as he felt fit. He was not going to move until he

The Hadley team. (Left to right), Peter Warwick (chairman), John Stanford (secretary), Rosemary Murray, Colin Smith and James Warwick (director)

had a piece of paper in his hands. As the cargo was U.S. Aid to Jordan, the Jordanian authorities adopted the attitude of why should they, in the circumstances, issue any certificate guaranteeing the cargo was for consumption within Jordan. In the event, however, reason prevailed, the Jordanian authorities relented and issued a certificate guaranteeing the cargo was for consumption within Jordan. The certificate was put on board an outward bound ship and delivered to the Commander of the SAMUEL S. ROBERTS. CLYMENE was allowed to continue her passage to Aqaba, where the cargo was discharged without further incident. In all the whole episode was a classic example of bureaucracy in action.

In 1987 the Company moved their offices out of Furness Building, 53 Leadenhall Street, London. After 61 years, they moved to new premises at Telford's Yard, 6-8, The Highway, Wapping, London, E.1., not too great a distance away. At this time Peter Warwick's son James entered the Company as the fifth generation of the family in the shipping industry. This move was necessitated by the decision of Furness Withy to relocate their own offices out of London, to Redhill, Surrey.

With a sustained upturn in the market it was decided, in 1991, that there was room for expansion in the fleet. Accordingly a second-hand Polish, Panamax-type bulk carrier, GENERAL ZAWADZKI, was purchased, at a cost of $12.5 million, and renamed CERINTHUS, bringing the fleet to four vessels. With continued changes in trade patterns the next re-appraisal of strength and viability saw CLARE sold in 1995 for further trading, her place in the fleet being taken by the 64,643 dwt Japanese built STARFEST.

Costing $11.4 million she entered the fleet as the second CAMARINA. By a narrow margin in length and deadweight when compared with CLYMENE she became the largest vessel in the fleet.

The current employment of the fleet is varied. CAMARINA and CERINTHUS are both on two year time charters. CAMARINA's commenced in February 1996, to the China Chartering Corporation, Beijing, for whom she has carried bauxite, grain and coal between ports in Europe, North America and the Far East. CERINTHUS is nearing the end of her charter, which commenced in February 1995, to Island View Shipping, Durban. In this employ she has also travelled widely, including ports in the Near, Middle and Far East, Australia, South Africa, Europe and Black Sea. Cargo has been varied, including grain, steel, coal, ore, etc. CLYMENE has recently been on voyage charters with grain. Their small sister COTINGA continues to operate under Everard management between British, European and Mediterranean ports with a variety of cargo including fertiliser, china clay, phosphate, coal, wheat and coke.

With the market in free fall around the middle of 1996 the Company was preparing for a lean time and the fleet was plying for trade worldwide.

Keeping it in the family. Peter Warwick's yacht is also named CLYMENE

On board CERINTHUS (3). Captain's day room (top), saloon (middle) and engine starting platform (bottom)

WAR JANDOLI (later CEPOLIS) entering Taranto 15 July 1920. Passing through the Canale Navigabile from Mar Grande to Mar Piccolo
(Shell Photographic Library)

FLEET LIST
&
APPENDIX

FLEET NOTES.

Due to the complexity of ownership and management of the vessels owned by Hadley Shipping Company Ltd and the associated Coastal Tankers Ltd, Iranian Tanker Company Ltd, Leadenhall Shipping Company Ltd and other companies, the following explanation may assist in clarifying the situation.

From the outset the fleet of Hadley Shipping has been managed by the Immingham Agency Company Ltd. Subsequently Coastal Tankers and the other companies placed their vessels under the management of Hadley Shipping, and therefore indirectly under the control of Immingham Agency.

During World War II the British Government placed vessels under the management of both Hadley Shipping and, more so, Coastal Tankers. Indirectly they were all managed by Immingham Agency and all occupied the same offices.

NOTES ON SHIP HISTORIES

The first line contains the chronological number for the ship, name and period in the fleet.

The second line contains the British official number (O.N.), gross, net and deadweight tonnages followed by registered dimensions (length, beam and depth), and type of vessel.

The third line details the type of engine, reciprocating (T=triple expansion, C=compound), turbine or diesel, number and sizes of cylinders and power, and manufacturers. S.C=stroke cycle, S.A.=single acting, D.A.=double acting, ihp=indicated horse power (reciprocating), nhp = nominal horse power, shp=shaft horse power (turbine) and bhp=brake horse power (diesel).

THE HADLEY SHIPPING COMPANY LTD.

1. CEPOLIS (1) (1926 - 1936)
O.N. 143048. 5,578g. 3,365n. 8,385d. 400.0 x 52.3 x 28.4 feet. Tanker.
T.3-cyl. (27", 44" & 73" x 48") 2,500 ihp engine manufactured by the shipbuilder.
3.6.1918: Keel laid by Swan, Hunter and Wigham Richardson Ltd, Newcastle (Yard No.1092), as the "Z" type standard WAR JANDOLI, for the Shipping Controller (Lane and Macandrew Ltd, London, managers), London. 31.12.1918: Launched. 3.1919: Completed. 20.3.1919: Delivered and employed initially as an Admiralty Fleet Oiler (chartered) or Mercantile Fleet Oiler (M.F.O.). 1920: Sold to the Anglo-Saxon Petroleum Company Ltd, London, delivered 16.4.1920 and renamed CEPOLIS. 1926: Purchased, for £60,000 by Hadley Shipping Company Ltd, London. 24.12.1926: Taken over. 1936: Sold, for £11,000, to shipbreakers at Yokohama. 2.1937: Demolition commenced.

CEPOLIS (1)   (F.W. Hawks)

2. CORATO (1) (1928 - 1938)
O.N. 142659. 5,563g. 3,476n. 8,435d. 400.0 x 52.4 x 28.5 feet.   Tanker.
T.3-cyl. (27", 44" & 73" x 48") 2,500 ihp engine manufactured by G. Clark Ltd, Sunderland.
29.8.1918: Launched by Sir J. Laing and Sons Ltd, Sunderland (Yard No. 672), as the "Z" type standard WAR JEMADAR, for the Shipping Controller (Hunting and Son, Newcastle, managers), London. 9.1918: Completed. Employed initially as an Admiralty Fleet Oiler (chartered) or Mercantile Fleet Oiler (M.F.O.). 1920: Sold to the Anglo-Saxon Petroleum Company Ltd, London, and delivered 5.2.1920. 1921: Renamed CLIONA. 1926: Sold to Deutsche Tankschiffreederei A.G., Hamburg. 1927: M. Morck appointed manager. 7.12.1928: Purchased, for £64,000, by Hadley Shipping Company Ltd, London. 5.4.1929: Renamed CORATO, registered initially at Singapore. 1929: Transferred to London registry. 1938: Sold for £10,500 to T.W. Ward Ltd, for demolition at Briton Ferry, with delivery during July 1938.

CERINTHUS (1)   *(WSPL)*

3. CERINTHUS (1) (1930 - 1942)
O.N. 162481. 3,878g. 2,318n. 5,875d. 336.0 x 48.8 x 25.6 feet.   Tanker.
T.3-cyl. (20", 33" & 55" x 39") 385 nhp engine manufactured by the shipbuilder.
23.8.1930: Launched by Hawthorn, Leslie and Company Ltd, Newcastle (Yard No.577), for £80,000, for Hadley Shipping Company Ltd, London. 9.1930: Completed. 20.12.1930: Delivered.   11.1934 until 3.1935: Laid up on the Tyne. 9.12.1942: Whilst on a ballast voyage from London and Oban to Freetown, was torpedoed and then shelled by the German submarine U128, under command of Kapitänleutnant Ulrich Heyse, S.W. from the Cape Verde Islands, and sank at a position 12.27N 27.45W. Of her compliment of 39 crew and gunners, 20 were lost.

4. BASSETHOUND (1934 - 1954)
O.N. 163454. 1,174g. 574n. 1,537d. 222.6 x 35.1 x 15.8 feet.   Tanker.
T.3-cyl. (16", 27" & 45" x 33") 116 nhp engine manufactured by D. Rowan and Company Ltd, Glasgow.
28.2.1934: Launched by the Blythswood Shipbuilding Company Ltd, Glasgow (Yard No.36), for £36,000, for Hadley Shipping Company Ltd, London. 4.4.1934: Completed. 8.1940: Requisitioned by The Ministry of Shipping, (later the Ministry of War Transport), and spent over three years as a fresh water supply vessel at Freetown. 10.1945: Returned to commercial service. 1954: Sold, for £14,000, to the Thames Welding Company Ltd, London. 1956: Sold to the Helmsman Shipping Company Ltd, (C. Rowbotham and Sons (Management) Ltd, managers), London, and renamed POINTSMAN. 10.1968: Scrappingco S.A., Brussels, commenced demolition at Antwerp.

BASSETHOUND   (FotoFlite)

5. JAMAICA PLANTER (1936 - 1940)

O.N. 164703. 4,098g. 2,407n. 356.6 x 50.2 x 29.7 feet.
Refrigerated cargo / 16 x 1st class passengers.
Two, 6-cyl. 2 S.C.S.A. (590 x 900mm) 2,000 bhp B&W type oil engines
manufactured by J.G. Kincaid and Company Ltd, Glasgow, geared to
twin screw shafts.
8.6.1936: Launched by Lithgows Ltd, Port Glasgow (Yard No.885), for
£152,000, for Hadley Shipping Company Ltd, London.   8.1936:
Completed. 31.10.1938 until 23.12.1938: At Copenhagen for engine tests
and modifications.   9.1940: Sold to the Jamaica Banana Producers'
Steamship Company Ltd, Kingston, Jamaica, (Kaye, Son and Company
Ltd, London, managers). 22.1.1941: Exploded a mine at a position
approximately 2,500 yards off Nell's Point, Barry Island, S. Wales, and
was beached in the Old Harbour, Barry. 13.2.1941: Refloated, and
beached in Whitmore Bay. 18.2.1941: Refloated, and docked at Barry for
repair. 1.7.1941: Damaged by aircraft bombs at Barry. 27.12.1944: Whilst
on a voyage from Halifax N.S. to Avonmouth, collided with the American
T.3 type tanker WELLESLEY 9,880/43 which was anchored in Barry Roads
in thick fog at a position 51.21N 03.14 W, and sank in 12 fathoms of
water. All her passengers and crew were picked up from three lifeboats
by SARNIA 711g./23 and landed at Barry.

JAMAICA PLANTER on trials   (W. Ralston)

63

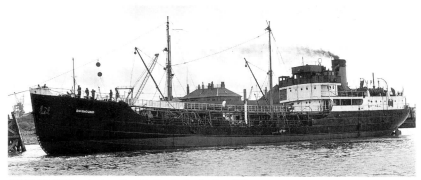

DAXHOUND entering Roath Basin lock, Cardiff
(Welsh Industrial & Maritime Museum)

6. DAXHOUND (2) (1939 - 1951)

O.N. 167225.　　1,128g. 529n. 1,500d.　227.3 x 36.2 x 13.2 feet.　Tanker.
Post 1953:　　　1,189g. 605n. 1,576d.
As built:　T.3-cyl. (17", 27-9/16" & 45-11/16" x 29-9/16") 194 nhp engine manufactured by A. Borsig G.m.b.H., Berlin / Tegel.
Post 1953: 6-cyl. 4 S.C.S.A. (400 x 460mm) 1,200 bhp M6V 40/46 oil engine manufactured in 1943 by Maschinenfabrik Augsburg-Nurnberg A.G., Augsburg, for the German submarine U 108.
5.9.1931: Launched as MITRA by Deutsche Werft Betrieb Finkenwerder, Hamburg (Yard No.152), for Dampskibs. Marna A/S., (Sigurd Owren, manager), Oslo. 10.1931: Completed. 3.1939: Purchased, for £41,000, by Hadley Shipping Company Ltd, London, and renamed DAXHOUND. 11.1951: Sold, for £78,000, to Carl W. Hanssen Tankschiffahrt, Hamburg, and renamed AMRUM. 1953: Re-engined. 1969: Sold to Compagnia di Navigazione Motia S.p.A. (S.Lucchese, manager), Venice, and renamed LUKI. 1970: Converted into a sludge carrier. 1988: Owners restyled as Motia S.p.A., and vessel sold for demolition.

CERINTHUS (2) alongside Rank's Mill, No 2 dock, Cardiff
(Welsh Industrial & Maritime Museum)

64

7. CERINTHUS (2) (1947 - 1951)

O.N. 169656. 7,265g. 4,454n. 10,940d. 423.9 x 57.0 x 34.8 feet.
T.3-cyl. (24", 37" & 70" x 48") 2,500 ihp engine manufactured by Harrisburg Machinery Corporation, Harrisburg, U.S.A.
25.9.1943: Launched as NIKOLA TESLA by Bethlehem Fairfield Shipyard Inc., Baltimore (Yard No. 2240), for the United States War Shipping Administration. 4.10.1943: Completed as SAMKANSA, for bareboat charter to the Ministry of War Transport (Orient Steam Navigation Company Ltd, managers), London. 1947: General Steam Navigation Company Ltd, London, appointed as managers. 17.4.1947: Purchased, for £135,000, by Hadley Shipping Company Ltd, London. 22.5.1947: Delivered and renamed CERINTHUS (chartered to Houlder Brothers and operated in their colours for the duration of ownership). 11.1951: Sold, for £580,000, to Rio Amado Compania Naviera S.A. (Capeside Steam Ship Company Ltd, London, managers), Panama, and renamed PHASSA. 1953: Sold to Compania de Naviera Cerro La Plata, (Coulothros Ltd, London, managers), Panama, and renamed URANIA. 1960: Syros Shipping Company (L.M. Valmas and Son) Ltd, appointed as managers. 1964: Sold to Evergreen Navigation Corp., Monrovia, (Wah Kwong and Company (Hong Kong) Ltd, Hong Kong, managers), Panama flag, and renamed CONCORD VENTURE. 10.1.1970: Arrived at Tadotsu for demolition by Miyachi Salvage Company Ltd.

CORATO (2) in Roath Basin, Cardiff   *(Welsh Industrial & Maritime Museum)*

8. CORATO (2) (1952 - 1962)

O.N. 184590. 11,387g. 6,489n. 16,636d. 523.9 x 69.3 x 38.5 feet. Tanker.
5-cyl. 2 S.C.S.A. (670 x 2320mm) 3,500 bhp Doxford type oil engine manufactured by Scott's Shipbuilding & Engineering Company Ltd, Greenock.
14.12.1951: Launched by Greenock Dockyard Company Ltd, Greenock (Yard No.477), for Hadley Shipping Company Ltd, London. 3.1952: Completed. 1962: Sold, for £97,500, to Compagnie d'Armement Maritime S.A., Djibouti, (Société de Travaux et Transports Maritimes S.A.R.L., Paris, managers), and renamed SENANQUE. 1965: Sold to Yugoslavian shipbreakers who resold to Spanish shipbreakers. 5.3.1965: Departed from Bordeaux, en route to Barcelona. 22.3.1965: Demolition commenced. 2.11.1965: Work completed.

CERINTHUS (3) – note the size of her funnel   *(WSPL)*

9. CERINTHUS (3) (1954 - 1976)
O.N. 186145. 12,174g. 7,149n. 19,180d. 530'0" x 69'5" x 29'8". Tanker.
Two steam turbines manufactured by the shipbuilder, reduction geared
to a single screw shaft. 8,250 shp.
29.6.1954: Launched by Harland and Wolff Ltd, Belfast (Yard No.1470),
for Hadley Shipping Company Ltd, London. 11.1954: Completed.
23.7.1976: Arrived at Faslane for demolition by Shipbreaking Industries
Ltd.

10. CLYMENE (1) (1961 - 1976)
O.N. 302675. 12,251g. 6,952n. 18,500d. 530'0" x 69'5" x 29'10". Tanker.
Two steam turbines manufactured by Hawthorn, Leslie (Engineers) Ltd,
Newcastle, reduction geared to a single screw shaft. 7,500 shp.
19.12.1960: Launched by Hawthorn, Leslie (Shipbuilders) Ltd, Hebburn
(Yard No.740), for Hadley Shipping Company Ltd, London. 7.1961:
Completed. 3.8.1976: Arrived at Kaohsiung for demolition by Nan Ying
Iron and Steel Works Company Ltd. 14.9.1976: Work commenced.

CLYMENE (1)   *(WSPL)*

11. CLYDESDALE (1967 - 1969)

O.N. 334651. 24,024g. 16,863n. 42,820d. 620'0" x 91'4" x 51'3".
Bulk Carrier.
6-cyl. 2 S.C.S.A. (900 x 1550mm) 13,810 bhp Scott-Sulzer 6RD90 type oil engine manufactured by the shipbuilder.
18.10.1965: Ordered from Scott's Shipbuilding & Engineering Company Ltd, Greenock (Yard No.707), for Hadley Shipping Company Ltd. 4.8.1966: Keel laid. 7.3.1967: Launched. 7.10.1967: Completed at a cost of £1,996,673, (£84,477 profit to builder) with ownership shared 32/64 Hadley Shipping Company Ltd., 22/64 Houlder Line Ltd, and 10/64

CLYDE BRIDGE proceeding down the St Lawrence, January 1972, after discharging sugar and sustaining bottom damage.

Empire Transport Company Ltd, all of London. 1969: Time chartered to Seabridge Shipping Ltd, and renamed CLYDE BRIDGE. 1972: Registered under Hadley Shipping Company Ltd. 1974: Sold to Houlder Brothers and Company Ltd (Warwick and Esplen Ltd, remaining managers), London. 28.1.1977: Allocated to Houlder Brothers' bulk shipping division, and renamed DUNSTER GRANGE. 12.2.1981: Sold to Stevinson, Hardy (Tankers) Ltd (Houlder Brothers and Company Ltd, managers), London. 1981: Furness, Withy (Shipping) Ltd, appointed as managers. 17.3.1982: Sold to Gulf Shipping Lines Ltd, Hong Kong (Waveney Marine Services Ltd, Ipswich, managers), and renamed GULF KESTREL. 3.1983: Gulfeast Ship Management Ltd, appointed managers. 1983: Sold to Graphite Shipping Inc. (same managers), Monrovia, and renamed FIVE STAR. 31.8.1986: Arrived at Kaohsiung for demolition by Nan Engineering Steel Company.

12. CLYDE BRIDGE (1969 - 1976) see ship No.11.

13. CAMARINA (1) (1969 - 1981)

O.N. 337854. 1,473g. 833n. 2,598d. 230'2" x 38'9" x 22'6".
8-cyl. 4 S.C.S.A. (320 x 450mm) 1,500 bhp, MaK 8M451AK type oil engine manufactured by Atlas-Mak Maschinenbau, Kiel.
30.4.1969: Launched by G. and W. Bodewes Scheepswerf N.V., Martenshoek (Yard No.502), for Hadley Shipping Company Ltd, London. 10.7.1969: Completed. 11.1981: Sold to Ikarian Star Shipping Company Ltd, Nicosia (N. Manolis, Piraeus, manager), and renamed NICOLAOS M II. 1990: Sold to Genimar Maritime Ltd (Kavomar Shipping Company, Piraeus, managers), St.Vincent, and renamed EVDOKIA II. 7.3.1991: Whilst on a voyage from Bourgas to Chioggia, with a cargo of steel coils, collided in dense fog with PHILIPPOS 1,598/54 in Chioggia Roads, and sank.

CAMARINA at Malta (W.J. Harvey)

14. CORATO (3) (1969 - 1978)

O.N. 337855. 1,476g. 832n. 2,640d. 230'2" x 38'9" x 22'6".
8-cyl. 4 S.C.S.A. (320 x 450mm) 1,500 bhp, MaK 8M451AK type oil engine manufactured by Atlas-Mak Maschinenbau, Kiel.
1.5.1969: Launched by N.V. Scheepswerf "Vooruitgang" (Gebrouder Suurmeyer), Foxhol (Yard No.223), for Hadley Shipping Company Ltd, London. 10.7.1969: Completed. 26.10.1978: Sold and delivered to "DARCO" Scheepvaart B.V. (Vertom Scheepvaart en Handelmaatschappij B.V., managers), Rotterdam, and renamed HARCO. 10.1980: Sold to Chr. M. Sarlis and Company M.C., Piraeus, and renamed PELLINI. 1987: Sold to Pellini Shipping Company S.A., Panama (Chr. M. Sarlis and Company M.C., Piraeus, managers). 1990: Sold to SFB Commercial and Shipping Company Ltd, Nicosia (Commercial and Shipping Company Ltd, Cairo, managers), and renamed NANCY SFB (St Vincent and the Grenadines registry). 1994: Sold to Kiwi Ltd (Malgache de Cabotage), Madagascar, and renamed ANTALAHA. 3.1995: Subsequent to her departure from Antsiranana, her classification was suspended due to her need of repairs and overdue surveys. Still in service.

CORATO (3) on trials (Fotobedrijf Piet Boonstra)

CALANDRIA   (FotoFlite)

15. CALANDRIA (1970 - 1979)
O.N. 338987. 1,477g. 832n. 2,598d. 230'2" x 38'9" x 22'6".
8-cyl. 4 S.C.S.A. (320 x 450mm) 1,500 bhp, MaK 8M451AK type oil engine manufactured by Atlas-Mak Maschinenbau, Kiel.
12.11.1969: Launched by G. and W. Bodewes Scheepsverf N.V., Martenshoek (Yard No.506), for Hadley Shipping Company Ltd, London.
3.1970: Completed. 8.1979: Sold to Lifeocean Compania Naviera S.A. (Fereniki Lines S.A., Piraeus), Panama, and renamed OUADAN. 6.4.1985: Laid up at Piraeus. 1986: Renamed FISKELA, Cypriot registry. 1986: Sold to Fiskela Shipping Company Ltd, Thessaloniki. 1989: Sold to Aquamarine Ltd, St Vincent (Fiskela Shipping Company Ltd, Thessaloniki, managers), and reverted to CALANDRIA. 1990: Sold to Qiong Xi Shipping Company Ltd, Haikou, China, and renamed QIONG XI. Still in service.

16. CUMBRIA (1971 - 1981)
O.N. 341485. 18,570g. 12,063n. 32,010d. 572'2" x 82'6" x 47'3".
Bulk carrier.
6-cyl. 2 S.C.S.A. (760 x 1550mm) 10,210 bhp Scott-Sulzer 6RD76 type oil engine manufactured by Scott's Engineering Company (1969) Ltd, Greenock.
20.6.1969: Ordered by unspecified Greek interests from Scott's Shipbuilding Company (1969) Ltd, Greenock (Yard No.720) and contract subsequently taken over by Hadley Shipping Company Ltd, London.
25.8.1970: Keel laid as CUMBRIA (the name CYMBELINE had been considered). 14.5.1971: Launched. 24.6.1971: Sea Trials. 1.7.1971: Delivered. 1981: Sold, for $12,999,000, to the USSR-Novorossiysk

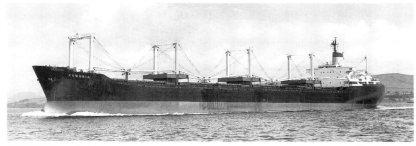

CUMBRIA on trials   *(W. Ralston)*

Shipping Company, Novorossiysk, Russia, and renamed DAGOMYS. 1990: Sold to Oriental Beauty S.A., Panama (Golden Union Shipping Company S.A., Piraeus, managers), and renamed FLAG PAOLA. 9.1979: reported sold Indian breakers.

17. CYMBELINE (1974 - 1984)
O.N. 308136.   5,513g. 2,779n. 7,975d.   112.78 x 16.36 x 7.640 metres.
5-cyl. 2 S.C.S.A. (560 x 1000mm) 3,860 bhp Sulzer 5RD56 type oil engine manufactured by Sulzer Bros Ltd, Winterthur.
23.11.1965: Launched as DALEWOOD by Bartram and Sons Ltd, Sunderland (Yard No.406), for William France, Fenwick and Company Ltd, London. 5.1966: Completed. 1972: Houlder Brothers and Company Ltd, London, appointed as managers. 1973: Sold to Allied Marine Facilities Ltd, London, (same managers). 1974: Purchased, for £850,000,

CYMBELINE   *(FotoFlite)*

70

by Hadley Shipping Company Ltd, and renamed CYMBELINE. 26.3.1984: Sold, for £145,000, to Garth Shipping Company Ltd (Idwal Williams and Company Ltd, managers), Cardiff, and renamed GREEN ROCK. 1985: Sold to Graig Shipping p.l.c. (same managers), Cardiff, and was proposed to be renamed COLUM but, after a period of lay-up, was returned to service as GREEN ROCK. 1986: Sold to Teambold Ltd, London, with the intention of renaming to ALBION S.A. 1986: Sold to Moonbeam Shipping (Capt. Pertsinis), Cyprus. 1986: Sold to Pipevine Ltd, London (Rockshire Shipping N.V., Curacao, managers), and renamed ROCKY. 1987: Sold to Rockshire Shipping Company N.V., Netherlands Antilles and Aruba. 26.12.1988: Whilst sheltering from heavy weather in Ashdod Harbour, was driven aground S. of Ashdod after her moorings had parted. Her crew was saved. Subsequently declared a constructive total loss.

COTINGA in the Nieuw Waterweg   *(W.J. Harvey)*

18. COTINGA (1976 -   )
O.N. 366301. 1,599g. 1,187n. 3,089d. 83.52 x 14.13 x 5.188 metres.
8-cyl. 4 S.C.S.A. (320 x 450mm) 2,400 bhp MaK 8M452AK type oil engine manufactured by Atlas-Mak Maschinenbau, Kiel.
10.9.1976: Launched by B.V. Bodewes Scheepsverf, Martenshoek (Yard No.528), for Hadley Shipping Company Ltd, London. 10.11.1976: Completed. 1986: F.T. Everard and Sons Management Ltd, appointed as managers.   In the present fleet.

19. CERINTHUS (4) (1978 - 1986)
O.N. 377546. 1,592g. 1,236n. 3,168d. 91.52 (BB) x 13.42 x 5.158 metres.
6-cyl. 4 S.C.S.A. (381 x 457mm) 2,650 bhp KMR6 type oil engine manufactured by Mirrlees Blackstone (Stockport) Ltd, Stockport.
5.3.1978: Launched by Appledore Shipbuilders Ltd, Appledore (Yard No. A.S. 120), for Hadley Shipping Company Ltd, London. 30.3.1978: Completed. 1986: Sold to Kavadas Shipping Company Ltd, Greece, and renamed TELIS K. 1986: Sold to Madriti Island Marine Company Ltd, Cyprus. 1992: Sold to Tunisian Sea Transport Company, Tunisia, and renamed JERBA.   Still in service.

20. CLYMENE (2) (1979 - 1986)
O.N. 386204. 5,999g. 3,283n. 7,923d. 121.85 x 17.61 x 7.711 metres.   Ice strengthened bulk carrier.
6-cyl. 2 S.C.S.A. (570 x 800mm) 5,325 bhp M.A.N. K6Z57/80F type oil engine manufactured by Maschinenbau Halberstadt, Halberstadt.

CERINTHUS (4) at Newport (W.J. Harvey)

9.4.1976: Launched as JOCARE by VEB Schiffswerft "Neptun", Rostock (Yard No.479), for Lars Rej Johansen, Norway. 31.8.1976: Completed. 1977: Sold to Compagnie de Nav. Mixte, Martinique, and renamed OYAPOK. 1978: Sold to Compagnie de Navale Chargeurs Delmas-Vieljeux (S.N.C.D.V.), France, and renamed BARBIZON. 1979: Purchased by Hadley Shipping Company Ltd, London, adapted for the carriage of newsprint in bulk, and renamed CLYMENE. 1986: Sold, for $1.5million, to Palmina Madre S.a.S., Italy, and renamed CHRIS. 1988: Sold to Blue Atlantic Maritime Ltd., Bahamas, and renamed B.A. CHRIS. 1990: Sold to South Molton Ltd (Tembo Shipping Ltd, managers), Bahamas, and

CLYMENE (2) in ballast, bound for the St Lawrence (FotoFlite)

72

renamed ALBA. 1993: Sold to Sun Glory Company Ltd (Zhi Cheng Maritime Ltd, Hong Kong, managers), and renamed SUN GLORY (St Vincent and the Grenadines registry). 1994: Sold to Accord Navigation Company Ltd, (same managers). Still in service.

CORATO (4) in the Falkland Islands

21. CORATO (4) (1983 - 1986)
O.N. 702176. 15,296g. 9,170n. 24,492d. 181.17(BB) x 22.86 x 10.197 metres. 6-cyl. 2 S.C.S.A. (760 x 1550mm) 12,000 bhp Sulzer 6RND76M type oil engine manufactured by H. Cegielski, Poznan.
1983: Completed as a bulk carrier. 1983: Converted to a trans-shipment storage bulk carrier. 1984: Reverted to a bulk carrier.
5.7.1982: Laid down by Georgi Dimitrov Shipyard, Varna (Yard No.150), for Nav. Maritime Bulgare, Bulgaria. Purchased on the stocks by Hadley Shipping Company Ltd, London. 24.9.1982: Launched. 30.6.1983: Completed, under Bermuda registry. 1986: Renamed CLARE, and transferred to Bahamas registry. 1994: Sold to Highway Shipping Company Ltd (Kapelco Maritime Services Ltd, managers), Cyprus, and renamed MATA K. Still in service.

22. CLARE (1986 - 1995) see ship No.21.

CLYMENE (3) in the English Channel   *(FotoFlite)*

23. CLYMENE (3) (1986 -   )

O.N. 712738. 31,077g. 22,124n. 60,194d. 222.99(BB) x 32.21 x 12.442 metres. Bulk carrier, strengthened for heavy cargoes.
6-cyl. 2 S.C.S.A. (760 x 1550mm) 14,400 bhp Sulzer 6RND76 type oil engine manufactured by Ishikawajima Harima Heavy Industries (I.H.I.), Aioi.
16.1.1981: Launched as ETERNITY VENTURE by China Shipbuilding Corp. (Keelung Division), Keelung (Yard No.180), for Triumph Carriers Inc. (Venture Shipping (Managers) Ltd, managers), Liberia. 10.4.1981: Completed. 1986: Sold to Prometheus Inc., Liberia, and renamed QUEEN NORA. 15.10.1986: Purchased by Hadley Shipping Company Ltd, London, and renamed CLYMENE, under Isle of Man registry. 1987: Transferred to Bahamian registry.   In the present fleet.

CERINTHUS (5)   (FotoFlite)

24. CERINTHUS (5) (1991 -   )

O.N. 716431. 23,406g. 13,343n. 40,009d. 198.56(BB) x 27.86 x 11.181 metres.   Bulk carrier.
6-cyl. 2 S.C.S.A.(680 x 1250mm) 10,800 bhp Sulzer 6RND68M type oil engine manufactured by H. Cegielski, Poznan.
12.10.1987: Launched as GENERAL ZAWADZKI by "Georgi Dimitrov" Shipyard, Varna (Yard No.081), for Polish Steamship Company (Polska Zegluga Morska), Poland.   25.3.1988: Completed. 1991: Purchased by Hadley Shipping Company Ltd, London, and renamed CERINTHUS, under Bahamian registry.   In the present fleet.

25. CAMARINA (2) (1995 -   )

O.N. 726407.   36,236g. 24,401n. 64,643d.   224.98(BB) x 32.26 x 12.820 metres.   Bulk carrier.
10-cyl. 4 S.C.S.A. (520 x 550mm) 10,550 bhp MAN 10V52/55A vee type oil engine manufactured by Mitsubishi Heavy Industries Ltd, Yokohama.
5.3.1982: Keel laid as YAMASHIRO MARU by Namura Shipbuilding Company Ltd, Imari (Yard No. 858), for Yamashita-Shinnihon Kisen K.K., Japan.   2.7.1982: Launched. 29.10.1982: Completed. 1989: Owners restyled as Yamashita-Shinnihon Steamship Company Ltd. 1990: Sold to Intermodal Shipping Inc. (Navix Ship Management Company Ltd, managers), Philippines, and renamed STARFEST. 1994: Sold to Cyr Transport and Marine Services Inc. (Jade Shipping Corp, managers), Philippines. 1995: Purchased by Hadley Shipping Company Ltd, London, and renamed CAMARINA.   In the present fleet.

CAMARINA (2) (FotoFlite)

Vessel chartered by
THE HADLEY SHIPPING COMPANY LTD.

HC.1. CORNELIA S / DAXHOUND (1) (1936 - 1938)

O.N. 165359. 977g. 576n. 197.8 x 32.8 x 15.4 feet. Tanker.
Post 1953: 1,153g. 716n. 221.1 x 32.8 x feet.
Two, 7-cyl. 4 S.C.S.A. (285 x 420mm) MAN type oil engines manufactured by Maschinenbau Augsburg-Nurnberg A.G., Augsburg, geared to a single screw shaft. 890 bhp.
Post 1955: Two, 8-cyl. 2 S.C.S.A. (285 x 420mm) oil engines manufactured by Maschinenfabrik Kiel A.G., Kiel.
5.9.1936: Launched as CORNELIA S by Werft Nobiskrug G.m.b.H., Rendsburg (Yard No.446), for Deutsche Fanto-Ges., Hamburg. 12.1936:

The chartered DAXHOUND (1) (WSPL)

75

Completed for Fanto Petroleum and Shipping Company Ltd, London, and chartered to Hadley Shipping Company Ltd (Immingham Agency Company Ltd, London, managers). 1.1937: Renamed DAXHOUND. 1938: Sold to N.V. Maatschappij Zeeschip "Frisia" (N.V. Phs. Van Ommeren's Scheepvaartbedrijf, managers), Holland, and renamed FRISIA. 1948: Sold to N.V. Verenigde Tankkustvaart, Holland. 1953: Sold to Jürgen Weitert Tankschiffreederei, W. Germany, lengthened, and renamed GUSTAV HEINRICH WEITERT. 1955: Owners restyled as Partreederei m.s. Gustav Heinrich Weitert (Jürgen Weitert Tankschiffreederei, managers), and vessel re-engined by U.and V. Norderwerft. 1956: Sold to Partenreederei m.s. Marxburg (Atlantic Reederei F. and W. Joch, managers), W. Germany, and renamed MARXBURG. 1960: Sold to Partenreederei m.s. Maya, (same managers), and renamed MAYA. 18.8.1965: Walter Ritscher commenced demolition at Hamburg.

Vessels managed by
THE HADLEY SHIPPING COMPANY LTD.

HM.1. EMPIRE GRANITE (1941 - 1943)
O.N. 164844. 8,028g. 4,677n. 463.5 x 61.2 x 33.0 feet.   Tanker.
T.3-cyl. (28", 46" & 76" x 51") 567 nhp engine manufactured in 1925 by Palmer's Ship Building and Iron Company Ltd, Jarrow. (This engine was removed from BRITISH INVENTOR 7,101g./26 which had broken in two and been broken up following a mine explosion in 1940.)
12.12.1940: Launched by Furness Shipbuilding Company Ltd, Haverton Hill-on-Tees (Yard No.326), for the Ministry of War Transport (Hadley Shipping Company Ltd, managers), London. 3.1941: Completed. 1943: Anglo-Saxon Petroleum Company Ltd, appointed as managers. 21.12.1945: Sold to Anglo-Saxon Petroleum Company Ltd, and in 1946 renamed KENNERLEYA. 1953: Transferred to Shell Company of Gibraltar Ltd, for employment as a storage hulk. 3.1960: Terrestre Marittima S.p.A., commenced demolition at La Spezia.

HM.2. EMPIRE AMETHYST (1941 - 1942)
O.N. 164848. 8,032g. 4,676n. 463.5 x 61.2 x 33.0 feet.   Tanker.
T.3-cyl. (27", 44" & 76" x 51") 674 nhp engine manufactured by Richardsons, Westgarth and Company Ltd, Hartlepool.
8.7.1941: Launched by Furness Shipbuilding Company Ltd, Haverton Hill-on-Tees (Yard No.330), for The Ministry of War Transport (Hadley Shipping Company Ltd, managers), London. 12.1941: Completed. 6.4.1942: Sailed from New Orleans, as an independent, bound to Freetown, Sierra Leone. 13.4.1942: 05:52 hrs sunk by the German submarine U 154, under command of Korvettenkapitän Walter Kolle, at a position 17.40N 74.50W. There were no survivors from her 41 crew and 6 gunners.

HM.3. RADBURY (1941 - 1944)

O.N. 136821. 3,614g. 2,276n. 360.2 x 50.3 x 21.5 feet.
T.3-cyl. (26", 42" & 68" x 42") 346 nhp engine manufactured by shipbuilders.
8.4.1910: Launched by William Doxford and Sons Ltd, Sunderland (Yard No.407), as IZRADA, for Navigazione Libera Giovanni Racich and Company, Austria - Hungary. 6.1910: Completed. 13.8.1914: Captured whilst homeward bound from Montevideo and Rosario, and taken into Mount's Bay, Penzance by the British Fishery Protection Cruiser SQUIRREL, thence to Falmouth the next day. Subsequently renamed POLDENNIS. 1916: Condemned as a War Prize and sold to Fisher, Alimonda and Company Ltd, London. 30.6.1917: Chased by an enemy submarine whilst in the Mediterranean but made good her escape by speed. 1921: Sold to Navigazione Libera Giovanni Racich and Company, Yugoslavia, and renamed IZRADA. 1926: Sold to Atlantska Plovidba Ivo Racic a.d., Yugoslavia. 1928: As a result of an amalgamation, owners restyled as Jugoslavenski Lloyd a.d., Yugoslavia. 1935: Sold to Brodarsko Akcionarsko Drustvo 'Oceania', Yugoslavia, and renamed BOR. 6.1941: Following the invasion of Yugoslavia many of the fleet were transferred to the Ministry of War Transport, and given names with RAD prefix's as the owner's London agents were Radonicich Ltd. The vessel was renamed RADBURY, (Hadley Shipping Company Ltd, managers). 10.8.1944: Sailed from Lourenco Marques with coal for Mombasa as an independent. 13.8.1944: Torpedoed and sunk at a position 24.20S 41.45E by the German submarine U 862 commanded by Korvettenkapitän Heirich Timm. 19 crew and 1 gunner were lost.

HM.4. EMPIRE SIMBA (1941 - 1945)

O.N. 168015. 5,691g. 3,403n. 409.6 x 54.2 x 27.1 feet.
Steam turbine manufactured by the General Electric Company, Schenectady, New York, reduction geared to screw shaft. 2,500 shp.
6.6.1918: Launched as WEST COHAS by Skinner and Eddy Corporation, Seattle, Washington (Yard No.24), for the United States Shipping Board. 1919: Completed. 1933: Sold to the Lykes Brothers-Ripley Steamship Company Inc., U.S.A. 1938: Transferred to the Lykes Brothers Steamship Company Inc., U.S.A. 10.8.1940: Purchased by the Ministry of Shipping, subsequently the Ministry of War Transport (Andrew Weir and Company, managers), London, and renamed EMPIRE SIMBA. 1.3.1941: Bombed at a position 52.21N 05.23W resulting in damage amidships and the engine and boiler rooms being flooded. Taken in tow and 4.3.1941 docked at Liverpool. 12.3.1941: Following an air raid at Liverpool a parachute mine was found on deck. The mine exploded 14.3.1941 causing further damage amidships. 26.3.1941: Discharge of cargo commenced and ship was subsequently repaired and returned to service, (Hadley Shipping Company Ltd, managers). 9.9.1945: Sailed from Loch Ryan with 500,000 obsolete mustard gas shells (8,032 tons). 13.9.1945: Scuttled in approximately 1,300 fathoms at a position 55.20N 11.00W, in the North Atlantic.

HM.5. EMPIRE COMMERCE (1943)

O.N. 169112. 3,722g. 1,993n. 343.5 x 48.3 x 26.5 feet.   Tanker.
3-cyl. 2 S.C.S.A. (600 x 2,320mm) 2,500 bhp oil engine manufactured by Wm. Doxford and Sons Ltd, Sunderland.
23.12.1942: Launched by Sir J. Laing and Sons Ltd, Sunderland, (Yard No.748), for the Ministry of War Transport, (Hadley Shipping Company

Ltd, managers), London. 4.1943: Completed. 9.1943: Ordered to join convoy MKS 26 from Bona to Algiers, in ballast, but having a foul bottom and fuel problems (she had been supplied with light gas oil instead of diesel) could only manage 7 knots with torpedo nets streamed. The convoy speed was 11 knots. Falling behind from her station (No.73 - the rear ship in the starboard wing column) the nets were hauled to catch up when, at 21:00 hrs. on 30th September 1943, a suspicious object was sighted on the starboard quarter. Ten minutes later a torpedo exploded in No.5 tank, starboard side. U 410, under command of Oberleutnant zür See Horst - Arno Fenski, had fired a spread of five torpedoes, hitting EMPIRE COMMERCE and FORT HOWE. Damage extended right across the ship, with the aft end slewed 10 degrees to starboard and the port side split right open. The crews of the two ships were shortly picked up by HMS ALISMA. The stern of EMPIRE COMMERCE soon broke off and sank at a position 37.19N., 06.40E. The forward section, picked up by a tug, was abandoned on fire off Phillipeville, to drift ashore 8 miles east of that town and burn out.

HM.6. EMPIRE GAIN (1943 - 1946)
O.N. 169121. 3,738g. 2,000n. 343.5 x 48.3 x 26.5 feet. Tanker. 3-cyl. 2 S.C.S.A. (600 x 2,320mm) 2,500 bhp oil engine manufactured by Wm. Doxford and Sons Ltd, Sunderland.
17.6.1943: Launched by Sir J. Laing and Sons Ltd, Sunderland, (Yard No.752) for The Ministry of War Transport, (Hadley Shipping Co.Ltd, managers). 9.1943: Completed. 1.5.1946: Sold to Anglo-Saxon Petroleum Company Ltd, London, and renamed BARBATIA. 1955: Owners restyled as Shell Petroleum Company Ltd. 11.1956: Seized by Egyptian military forces, and had a Russian Captain installed. 11.10.1957: Allocated to the Egyptian General Petroleum Organisation, Egypt, and renamed MAGD. 1961: Transferred to the United Arab Maritime Company, Egypt. 6.1967: Sunk in the Suez Canal, by aircraft during the Arab-Israeli "six day war". During October / November 1974, the wreck was lifted in sections by the Merritt Division of the Murphy Pacific Marine Salvage Corporation of New York, and dispersed along with the wrecks of nine other vessels.

HM.7. EMPIRE JUMNA (1945 - 1946)
O.N. 180361. 2,730g. 1,281n. 291.0 x 44.0 x 19.1 feet. Tanker. T.3-cyl. (18" 31" & 52" x 39") engine manufactured by D. Rowan and Company Ltd, Glasgow.
31.10.1944: Launched by Grangemouth Dockyard Company Ltd, Grangemouth, (Yard No. 458), for the Ministry of War Transport, (Hadley Shipping Company Ltd, managers), London. 1.1945: Completed. 1946: Owners restyled the Ministry of Transport. 17.4.1946: Sold to Anglo Saxon-Petroleum Company Ltd, London, and renamed FOSSULARCA. 1955: Owners restyled Shell Petroleum Company Ltd. 1960: Transferred to Shell tankers Ltd. 25.4.1962: Laid up at Singapore. 1964: Demolished by Hong Huat Ltd, Singapore.

HM.8. EMPIRE TEGEDEN (1945 - 1946)
O.N. 180721. 2,579g. 1,233n. 297.7 x 45.3 x 23.5 feet. Tanker. Two, oil engines (type and size unspecified) 3,500 bhp, manufactured by Schichau-Sulzer.
8.6.1938: Launched as JEVERLAND by Howaldtswerke A.G., Hamburg, (Yard No.782), a sub-contract from Neptun Werft, Rostock. 16.6.1938:

Arrived under tow at Rostock for completion as Neptun Werft, (Yard No.491), for unspecified owners, but work was suspended due to lack of special materials. 5.1941: Towed to Copenhagen for completion by Burmeister and Wain. 5.1942: Completed for the Kriegsmarine, (Atlantic Rhederei F. and W. Joch, Hamburg, managers). 5.1942: In service as a supply tanker at the Naval base at Kiel. 5.1945: Taken by the Allied Authorities at Bergen and allocated to the Ministry of War Transport, London, (Hadley Shipping Company Ltd, appointed as managers), and renamed EMPIRE TEGEDEN. 9.11.1945: Arrived at Methil from lay-up at Copenhagen. 1946: Owners restyled the Ministry of Transport. 26.7.1946: Sold to the Government of Russia, renamed FEOLENT, and up to 1959, due to the lack of information no new details had been added when Lloyd's Register deleted the entry, although one other source states that vessel was still employed in the Baltic during 1981.

VRISSI, ex EMPIRE TAGINDA   *(WSPL)*

HM.9. EMPIRE TAGINDA (1945 - 1947)
O.N. 180724. 3,227g. 1,612n. 328.9 x 45.7 x 23.9 feet.   Tanker.
Post 1934:   3,847g. 1993n.   377.4 x 45.7 x 23.9 feet.
T.3-cyl. (800, 970 & 1,575 x 1,050mm) 1,450 ihp engine manufactured by the shipbuilder.
8.4.1922: Launched by F. Krupp A.G. 'Germaniawerft', Kiel, (Yard No.414), as RUDOLF ALBRECHT for Mineralölwerke Albrecht and Company, Hamburg. 6.1922: Completed. 1931: Dr. Max Albrecht became manager. 1934: Lengthened by the shipbuilder. 1935: Sold to Partenreederi D. Rudolf Albrecht, (Dr. Max Albrecht, manager), Hamburg. 6.1945: Taken as war reparations by the British Authorities at Kiel and allocated to the Ministry of War Transport, (Hadley Shipping Company Ltd, managers), and renamed EMPIRE TAGINDA, (EMPIRE GASKET was also considered). 1946: Owners restyled the Ministry of Transport. 10.6.1947: Sold to Salvedor Company Ltd, (F. Bauer and Company Ltd., managers), London, and renamed BASINGSTREAM. 1949: Sold to Sojozita S.S. Company Ltd, (Ships Finance and Management Company Ltd, managers), London, and renamed OILSTREAM. 1952: Sold to Nicolas G. Nicolaou, Greece, and renamed VRISSI. 1953: Sold to C.G. Stergiopoulos, Greece. 15.11.1960: Arrived at La Spezia for demolition, by Celestri and Ci. S.p.A.

HM.10. EMPIRE JEWEL (1945 - 1946)

O.N. 180365. 2,730g. 1,281n. 291.0 x 44.0 x 19.1 feet. Tanker. T.3-cyl. (18" 31" & 52" x 39") engine manufactured by D. Rowan and Company Ltd, Glasgow.

12.6.1945: Launched by Grangemouth Dockyard Company Ltd, Grangemouth, (Yard No. 462), for The Ministry of War Transport, (Hadley Shipping Company Ltd, managers). 9.1945: Completed. 1946: Owners restyled the Ministry of Transport, (Coastal Tankers Ltd, managers). 29.4.1946: Sold to Anglo-Saxon Petroleum Company Ltd, London, and renamed FOSSARUS. 1956: Owners restyled Shell Petroleum Company Ltd. 25.9.1957: Laid up at Singapore. 24.10.1960: Hong Huat Ltd, commenced demolition at Singapore.

HM.11. EMPIRE TAGRALIA (1945 - 1947)

O.N. 180725. 5,824g. 3,474n. 385.0 x 55.1 x 32.0 feet. Tanker. Two, 6-cyl. 4 S.C.S.A. (570 x 1000mm) oil engines manufactured by the shipbuilder, geared to twin screw shafts. 3,600 bhp.

17.11.1928: Launched by Kockums M/V A/B., Malmo, (Yard No.158), as MAX ALBRECHT, for Partenreederei Max Albrecht, (Mineralölwerke Albrecht and Company managers), Hamburg. 1.1929: Completed. 1931: Sold to Mineralölwerke Albrecht Company G.m.b.H., (Dr. Max Albrecht, manager), Hamburg. 1935: Owners restyled as Albrecht Gebruder Company Komm-Ges.Hamburg. 3.9.1939: Interned at El Ferrol. 5.1945: Taken over by the British Authorities at El Ferrol. 11.10.1945: Allocated to the Ministry of War Transport, (Hadley Shipping Company Ltd, managers), and renamed EMPIRE TAGRALIA. 1946: Owners restyled the Ministry of Transport. 14.2.1947: Sold to the Basra Steam Shipping Company Ltd, (Galbraith, Pembroke and Company Ltd, managers), London, and renamed REPTON. 1.1952: Basra Steamship Company Ltd, sold to Idwal Williams and Company Ltd, Cardiff. 3.1952: Sold to Lloyd Siciliano Di Armamento S.p.A., Italy, and renamed ALCANTARA. 2.1957: Transferred to the A.G.I.P. Group S.p.A., Italy. 22.9.1959: Laid up at Genoa. 3.1960: Sold to A.R.D.E.M., of Genoa, for demolition. 9.1960: Demolition commenced at Vado Ligure.

HM.12. EMPIRE TEGLEONE (1945 - 1954)

O.N. 180745. 782g. 395n. 210.5 x 31.8 x 11.9 feet. Tanker. 5-cyl. 2 S.C.S.A. (340 x 570mm) 865 bhp Polar type oil engine manufactured by A/B Atlas Diesel, Skarhamn.

1942: Launched by Sarpsborg Mek.Verksted A/S, Greaker, (Yard No.12), as MARSTEINEN for Richard Jacobsen, Drobak, Norway. 1.2.1942: Purchased by Carl W. Hansen, Hamburg, on behalf of the Kriegsmarine, for employment as a supply tanker. 28.4.1942: Completed. 5.1945: Taken by the Allied Authorities at Copenhagen and allocated to the Ministry of War Transport, London. 2.8.1945: Arrived at Methil, Hadley Shipping Company Ltd, appointed as managers, and renamed EMPIRE TEGLEONE. 1946: Owners restyled the Ministry of Transport. 1954: Sold to Karl Herbert Beiser, (Leth and Company, managers), West Germany, and renamed OTTO. 1967: Sold to Seka S.A., Greece, and renamed KALI LIMENES II. 1982: Owners restyled as Sekavin Shipping Company. 1992: Sold to Vostistis Shipping Company, Greece, and renamed PUMA, under Honduran registry.

OTTO, ex EMPIRE TEGLEONE (WSPL)

HM.13. EMPIRE CROSS (1945 -1946)
O.N. 181112. 3,734g. 1,984n.   343.5 x 48.3 x 26.5 feet.   Tanker.
3-cyl. 2 S.C.S.A. (600 x 2,320mm) 2,500 ihp oil engine manufactured by
Wm. Doxford and Sons Ltd, Sunderland.
28.6.1945: Launched by Sir.J. Laing and Sons Ltd, Sunderland, (Yard No.
765), for the Ministry of War Transport, (Anglo-Saxon Petroleum
Company Ltd, managers). 11.1945: Completed. 1945: Hadley Shipping
Company Ltd, appointed managers. 1946: Owners restyled the Ministry
of Transport. 18.7.I946: Sold to Anglo-Saxon Petroleum Company Ltd,
London, who intended renaming the vessel BALEA, but, at 23:22 hours,
2.8.1946 still as EMPIRE CROSS, she suffered an explosion whilst
discharging aviation spirit at Haifa anchorage. The ship capsized and
sank in two minutes. 35 crew, including her Master, were saved by the
British destroyers VIRAGO and VENUS, together with various launches,
one of which was burnt out and sank. In total 9 British officers; 12 Lascar
sailors and 4 local Arab labourers were lost in the explosion. At the time
of the explosion there was 1,600 tons of 100 octane aviation spirit in her
tanks. A subsequent inquiry declared that the explosion had been from
accidental causes. The wreck was not considered worth salving and was
subsequently raised in 1952 and broken up by the Mediterranean
Salvage Company.

HM.14. NORD ATLANTIC (1945 - 1948)
O.N. 182683. 9,897g. 5,884n.   484.5 x 65.9 x 36.0 feet.   Tanker.
6-cyl. 2 S.C.D.A. (600 x 1100mm) 4,100 bhp oil engine manufactured by
Maschinenfabrik Augsburg-Nurnberg A.G., Augsburg.
23.12.1937: Launched by Deutsche Werft A.G., Betrieb Finkenwerder,
Hamburg, (Yard No.175), for John T. Essberger, Hamburg. 1.1938:
Completed. 5.8.1943: Stranded on the Spanish Coast whilst running the
Allied blockade but was later salvaged, towed to El Ferrol, and interned.
5.1945: Taken as a War Prize and allocated to the Ministry of War
Transport. It had been considered renaming the vessel NORD EST II,
but she was towed without name change to Portsmouth and Hadley
Shipping Company Ltd, appointed as managers. I946: Owners restyled
the Ministry of Transport. 11.1948: Sold to the South Georgia Company
Ltd, (Christian Salvesen and Company Ltd, managers), Leith, and
renamed SOUTHERN ATLANTIC. 10.1955: Sold to Schulte and Bruns
K.G., W. Germany.   1956: Converted into an ore carrier, by
Howaldswerke, Hamburg, and renamed CAROLA SCHULTE. 3.1.1972:
Laid up at Emden. 18.9.1972: Arrived in tow, at Bilbao for demolition.
10.1972: Revalirizacion de Materials S.A., commenced work.

CAROLA SCHULTE, ex NORD ATLANTIC (WSPL)

HM.15. FORT ST. PAUL (1946 - 1950)

O.N. 168484. 7,137g. 4,242n. 424.7 x 57.2 x 34.9 feet.
T.3-cyl. (24", 37" & 70" x 48") 2,500 ihp engine manufactured by J. Inglis and Company Ltd, Toronto..
26.12.1942: Launched by Marine Industries Ltd, Sorel, Quebec, (Yard No. 110), for the Government of the Dominion of Canada, and bareboat chartered to the Ministry of War Transport, (Maclay and McIntyre Ltd, Glasgow, managers). 5.1943: Completed. 1946: Charterers restyled the Ministry of Transport, (Hadley Shipping Company Ltd, appointed as managers), and at this point the ship was taken into the operations of the Houlder Line, on their United Kingdom - River Plate service, and was painted in their funnel colours. 1950: Charter period completed, and ship sold to Champlain Freighters Ltd., (J.P. Hadoulis Ltd, manager), London, and 1951 renamed TARSIAN. 1956: Sold to Marolas S.A., Liberia, and renamed MARIKA. 7.1958: Sold to the Peninsular Shipping Company Ltd, Hong Kong, and renamed LONGFORD. 1958: Sold to the Government of the Peoples Republic of China, and renamed HO PING WU SHI, (HO PING 50). 1967: The Bureau of Maritime Transport Administration, Shanghai Branch became managers, and ship renamed ZHAN DOU 50. 11.1991: Lloyd's Register deleted entry due to lack of up to date information and the fact that her callsign had been re-used on a more modern vessel of a different name.

FORT ST PAUL (WSPL)

HM.16. WAVE DUKE (1946 - 1948)

O.N. 180153. 8,199g. 4,644n.   473.0 x 64.1 x 35.6 feet.   Tanker.
Two steam turbines manufactured by Metropolitan Vickers Electric Company Ltd, Manchester, reduction geared to a single screw shaft.
16.11.1944: Launched as EMPIRE MARS by Sir J. Laing and Sons Ltd, Sunderland, (Yard No.755), for the Ministry of War Transport (British Tanker Company Ltd, managers). 4.1945: Completed. 10.1.1946: Sold to the Admiralty, (Hadley Shipping Company Ltd, appointed as managers), and renamed WAVE DUKE.   27.1.1948: Management ceased. 1964: Owners restyled as the Secretary of State for Defence (Naval Department), Royal Fleet Auxiliary service appointed as managers. 25.12.1969: Arrived in tow at Bilbao, from Plymouth to be demolished.

HM.17. WAVE LIBERATOR (1946 - 1948)

O.N. 169143. 8,135g. 4,634n.   473.8 x 64.3 x 35.4 feet.   Tanker.
Two steam turbines manufactured by Richardsons, Westgarth and Company Ltd, Hartlepool, reduction geared to a single screw shaft.
9.2.1944: Launched as EMPIRE MILNER by the Furness Shipbuilding Company Ltd, Haverton Hill-on- Tees, (Yard No. 358), for the Ministry of War Transport, (Anglo-Saxon Petroleum Company Ltd, managers). 6.1944: Completed. 1945: British Tanker Company Ltd, appointed as managers. 10.1.1946: Sold to the Admiralty, (Hadley Shipping Company Ltd, appointed as managers), and renamed WAVE LIBERATOR. 10.1.1948: Management ceased. 2.5.1959: Arrived at Hong Kong, under tow of GOLDEN CAPE 525g./42. 4.5.1959: The Hong Kong Salvage and Towage Company Ltd, commenced demolition.

COASTAL TANKERS LTD.

C.1. OTTERHOUND (1933 - 1950)
O.N. 149879. 860g. 403n. 190.5 x 32.5 x 14.6 feet. Tanker.
T.3-cyl. (16", 27" & 44" x 30") engine manufactured by Richardsons, Westgarth and Company Ltd, Middlesbrough.
12.7.1927: Launched by Furness Shipbuilding Company Ltd, Haverton Hill-on-Tees (Yard No.121), for Coastal Tankers Ltd, London. 8.1927: Completed. 1931: Immingham Agency Company Ltd, appointed managers. 1950: Sold to Irving Steamships Ltd, Canada. 1951: Sold to Kent Line Ltd, Canada. 1953: Reverted to Irving Steamships Ltd, Canada. 1952: Laid up with surveys overdue. 6.1955: Class expunged for non-compliance with regulations. c16.1.1960: Capsized and partially sank at her lay up berth, at St John N.B., subsequently broke away from shore and disappeared.

OTTERHOUND. Note the dog on the funnel band   *(WSPL)*

C.2. GOLDDRIFT (1951 - 1952)
O.N. 162720. 178g. 126n. 94.5 x 22.8 x 8.8 ft. Motor barge.
Post 1949: 199g. 97n. 96.6 x 22.8 x 8.8 ft.
Two, 2-cyl. 2 S.C.S.A. (8" x 9-1/16") oil engines manufactured by AB J. och C.G. Bolinders Mekaniska Verksted, Stockholm, connected to twin screw shafts. 52 nhp total.
Post 1949: 3-cyl. 2 S.C.S.A. (265 x 345mm) 350 bhp oil engine manufactured by Crossley Bros. Ltd, Manchester, geared to a single screw shaft.
19.8.1932: Launched by J. Pollock, Sons and Company Ltd, Faversham (Yard No.1408), for E.J. and W. Goldsmith Ltd, London. 1932: Completed. 1949: Lengthened and re-engined 1951: Sold to Coastal Tankers Ltd (Springwell Shipping Company Ltd, managers). 1952: Sold to G., J. and T. Gudmundsen, (T. Gudmundsen, manager), Norway, and renamed SULESKJAER. 1953: Owners restyled as T. Gudmundsen and Others. 1.10.1955: Whilst on a voyage from Brevik to Bergen, encountered severe weather conditions which caused her cargo to shift. She foundered off Jaeren, south of Stavanger.

GOLDDRIFT

C.3. GOLDEVE (1951 - 1952)

O.N. 163299. 178g. 126n. 94.5 x 22.8 x 8.8 ft. Motor barge.
Post 1949: 199g. 97n. 96.6 x 22.8 x 8.8 ft.
Two, 2-cyl. 2 S.C.S.A. (8"x 9-1/16") oil engines manufactured by by AB J. och C.G. Bolinders Mekaniska Verksted, Stockholm, connected to twin screw shafts. 52 nhp total.
Post 1949: 3-cyl. 2 S.C.S.A. (265 x 345mm) 225 bhp oil engine manufactured by Crossley Bros Ltd, Manchester, geared to a single screw shaft.
15.9.1932: Launched by J. Pollock, Sons and Company Ltd, Faversham (Yard No.1409), for E.J. and W. Goldsmith Ltd, London. 11.1932: Completed. 1949: Lengthened and re-engined. 1951: Sold to Coastal Tankers Ltd (Springwell Shipping Company Ltd, managers). 1952: Sold to Leadenhall Shipping Company Ltd (same managers), London, and renamed LEASPRAY. 1954: Immingham Agency Company Ltd appointed managers. 1956: Sold to Vectis Shipping Company Ltd. 1958: Sold to Sully and Company Ltd, Bridgewater. 1966: Sold to Light Shipping Company Ltd (Ross and Marshall Ltd, managers), Glasgow, and renamed WARLIGHT. 1972: Sold to Taylor, Woodrow Construction Ltd, London, and renamed TEAMWORK. 1976: Sold for demolition.

C.4. GOLDFAUN (1951 - 1952)

O.N. 164907. 319g. 163n. 390d. 133.8 x 24.7 x 7.5 feet.
6-cyl. 2 S.C.S.A. (265 x 345mm) 350 bhp, oil engine manufactured by Crossley Bros Ltd, Manchester.
9.5.1940: Launched as FIDDOWN by Goole Shipbuilding and Repairing Company Ltd, Goole (Yard No. 350), for Samuel Morris Ltd, Waterford, but vessel registered at Goole. 7.1940: Completed. 29.11.1940: Run down and sunk by the British destroyer HMS CAMPBELTOWN when entering the River Mersey. 7.7.1942: Raised and beached at Tranmere. 10.7.1942: Refloated, subsequently repaired. 1943: Taken over by the Ministry of War Transport, London (Craggs and Jenkins Ltd, Hull appointed managers), and renamed EMPIRE ESTUARY. 31.8.1946: Sold to E.J. and W. Goldsmith Ltd, London, and renamed GOLDFAUN. 1951: Sold to Coastal Tankers Ltd (Springwell Shipping Company Ltd, managers), London. 1952: Sold to Short Sea Shipping Company Ltd (same managers), London, and renamed CREEKDAWN. 7.1954: Sold to James

Tyrrell, Arklow, and renamed MURELL. 2.1972: Sold to Hammond Lane Metal Ltd, Dublin for demolition. 3.1972: Work completed.

GOLDFAUN   (WSPL)

C.5. GOLDGNOME (1951)
O.N. 167407. 288g. 140n. 370d. 126.4 x 23.5 x 7.3 ft.
Post 1964;   290g. 140n. 345d.
4-cyl. 2 S.C.S.A. (9-7/16" x 14-3/16") 200 bhp oil engine manufactured by Appingedammer Brons Motorenfabriek N.V., Appingedam.
Post 1954: 4-cyl. 2 S.C.S.A. (265 x 345mm) 345 bhp oil engine manufactured by Crossley Bros Ltd, Manchester.
Post 1964: 6-cyl. 4 S.C.S.A. (6" x 7") 300 bhp oil engine manufactured by Bergius-Kelvin Company Ltd, Glasgow.
9.3.1939: Launched as PALLAS by N.V. Scheepswerf Delfzijl v/h Gebr. Sander, Delfzijl (Yard No.158), for N. Engelsman, Delfzijl. 4.1939: Completed. 1940: Taken over by the Ministry of War Transport (W.A. Savage Ltd, Liverpool, managers), and renamed EMPIRE TULIP. 1945: Ross and Marshall Ltd, Greenock, appointed managers. 1946: Owners restyled as the Ministry of Transport. 1946: T.G. Irving, Sunderland appointed managers. 1947: Sold to E.J. and W. Goldsmith Ltd, London, and renamed GOLDGNOME. 1951: Purchased by Coastal Tankers Ltd. 1951: Sold to London and Rochester Trading Company Ltd, Rochester, and renamed INSISTENCE. 1954: Re-engined. 11.1964: Re-engined. 3.1970 Sold for demolition, minus her engine which was re-installed in owners tug DRAGGETTE 50g./1947. 12.1970 Remains of hull demolished at Rochester.

C.6. GOLDHIND (1951 - 1952)
O.N. 183002. 553g. 255n. 620d. 168.3 x 30.1 x 8.2 feet.
8-cyl. 2 S.C.S.A. (265 x 345mm) 480 bhp oil engine manufactured, in 1945, by Crossley Bros Ltd, Manchester.
Originally one of four 160 feet, twin screw auxiliary vessels ordered by the Admiralty (Fleet Air Arm) from J. Pollock, Sons and Company Ltd, Faversham, for the purpose of ferrying aircraft and aviation stores between aircraft carriers and shore establishments. To have been named SEA HURRICANE this order was cancelled in 1947 and the partly constructed hull sold to E.J. and W. Goldsmith Ltd, London, radically rebuilt, converted to single engine and lengthened. 18.12.1948: Launched as GOLDHIND (Yard No. 1844). 9.1949: Completed. 1951:

Purchased by Coastal Tankers Ltd (Immingham Agency Company Ltd, managers), London. 1952: Renamed PURPLE EMPEROR, (Springwell Shipping Company Ltd, appointed as managers). 1955: Sold to Anchor Shipping and Foundry Company Ltd, New Zealand, and renamed TOWAI. 1969: Sold to Southern Cross Shipping Pty Ltd, New Zealand, and renamed AKANA. 1970: Sold to Akana Pty Ltd (Hetherington Kingsbury Pty Ltd, managers), New Zealand. 1972: Sold to Hetherington Kingsbury Pty Ltd. 1973: Sold to Stannard Bros Holdings, New Zealand. 1974: Sold to Coastal Tug and Barge Pty Ltd, Port Moresby. 1975: Sold to Seafreight Pty Ltd, Port Moresby. 1977: Sold to Ali Ahamed, Maldives, and renamed MINAA MAAREE. 1979: Sold to D.I. Kalayfaanu, Maldives, and renamed MASAHI. 1985: Sold to D. Ibrahim Kalegefanu, Maldives. (possibly an amendment of name-spelling) 1995: Believed to be still in service, still in Lloyd's Register.

C.7. PURPLE EMPEROR (1952 - 1955) see ship No. C.6.

GOLDHIND   (WSPL)

C.8. CEPOLIS (2) (1955 - 1957)
O.N. 186208. 197g. 122n. 109'2" x 20'10" x 8'6".
3-cyl. 4 S.C.S.A. (280 x 450mm) 180 bhp oil engine manufactured by Deutz Motorenfabrik, Koln-Deutz.
Post 1971: 6-cyl. 4 S.C.S.A. (130 x 150mm) 270 bhp, TAMD120A type oil engine manufactured by A/B. Volvo-Penta, Gothenburg.
1927: Completed as JANTJE R by J. Koster Hzn, 'De Gideon', Groningen, (Yard No.109), for N.V. Motorschip 'Jantje R', Holland. 1934: Sold to Berend Bosma, Groningen, Holland, and renamed BEBO. 1945: Sold to J. Buisman, Holland 1950: Sold to G. Gruefeld, Holland, and renamed SOBAT. 1955: Sold to Esplen Trust Ltd, London, and renamed CEPOLIS. 1955: Purchased by Coastal Tankers Ltd (Immingham Agency Company Ltd, managers), London. 1957: Sold to Christian Moller, Denmark, and renamed KAMA. 1967: Sold to A.V. Madsen, Denmark, and renamed MOM. 1971: Re-engined. 1975: Sold to Y. Ally, A. Mazaharally and Sons Ltd, Guyana. c1988 - 1990: Sold to John Van Sluytman, Guyana. 1994: Reported as having been demolished.

Vessels managed by
COASTAL TANKERS LTD.

CM.1. EMPIRE MAIDEN (1942 - 1943)
O.N. 168705. 813g. 333n. 193.0 x 30.7 x 13.8 feet.   Tanker.
As built: T.3-cyl. (15″, 25½″ & 41″ x 30″) engine manufactured by D. Rowan and Company Ltd, Glasgow.
Post 1948: C.2-cyl. (430 & 900 x 550mm) 400 ihp engine manufactured in 1941, by Odero Terni Orlando, Leghorn.
Post 1962: 8-cyl. 4 S.C.S.A. (320 x 580mm) 1,050 bhp oil engine manufactured by Motorenwerke Mannheim A.G. (MWM), Mannheim.
20.12.1941: Launched by A. and J. Inglis Ltd., Glasgow, (Yard No.1151P), for the Ministry of War Transport, (Coastal Tankers Ltd, managers), London. 10.3.1942: Completed. 14.6.1943: Whilst on a voyage from Susa to Pantellaria with water, was sunk by aircraft bombs near Pantellaria Island. 17.4.1944: Raised and beached at Pantellaria where surveyors made an estimated requirement of at least ten weeks fair weather to complete work to make the vessel seaworthy for towing to a repair yard. 1948: Wreck purchased by Giovanni Dagnino, Italy. 10/11.6.1948: Wreck finally refloated. 7.7.1948: Arrived in tow at Messina, for temporary repairs. 7.8.1948: Departed in tow bound to Genoa for permanent repairs, including re-engining. 1952: Sold to Astrolea Societa Anon., Italy, and renamed ASTERIA. 1958: Sold to Cia. Trasporti Marittimi S.p.A. Nav., Italy, and renamed SANJACOPO. 1958: Sold to Lugari and Filippi, Italy. 1962: Sold to Societa Toscana di Armamanto e Navigazione S.r.L., Italy, and re-engined. 1972: Sold to Lidia Melodia Ved Lugari, Italy. 2.7.1974: Condi Homed Power Company, commenced demolition at La Spezia.

CM.2. EMPIRE HARP (1) (1942 - 1945)
O.N. 168779. 861g. 362n. 1,057d. 188.7 x 31.3 x 14.0 feet.   Tanker.
Post 1956:   983g. 466n. 210.0 x 31.3 x 14.0 feet.
T.3-cyl. (15″, 25″ & 42″ x 27″) 750 ihp engine manufactured by Amos and Smith Ltd, Hull.
22.11.1941: Launched by Goole Shipbuilding and Repairing Company Ltd, Goole, (Yard No.371), for the Ministry of War Transport, (Coastal Tankers Ltd, managers), London. 3.1942: Completed. 1946: Owner restyled the Ministry of Transport, (Anglo-Saxon Petroleum Company Ltd, managers). 1946: Coastal Tankers Ltd, appointed as managers. 25.11.1947: Sold to the Kuwait Oil Company Ltd, London, and 1948 renamed ANIS. 1954: Sold to F.T. Everard and Sons Ltd, London, and renamed AUTHENTICITY. 1956: Lengthened. 1966: Sold to Margarita Shipping and Trading Corp., (John S. Latsis, manager), Greece, and renamed PETROLA 1. 1969: Sold to Spyros J. Latsis, (same manager). 1977: Sold to Maritime and Commercial Company Argonaftis S.A., (same manager), Greece. 1984: Bilinder Marine Corp. S.A., became managers. 9.1984: Halivdeboeiki E.P.E., commenced demolition, at Aspropyrgos, Greece.

EMPIRE FAUN   (WSPL)

CM.3. EMPIRE FAUN (1943 - 1946)
O.N. 169080.   846g.   364n.   188.7 x 31.3 x 14.0 feet.   Tanker.
T.3-cyl. (15", 25" & 42" x 27") 750 ihp engine manufactured by Amos and Smith Ltd, Hull.
10.12.1942: Launched by the Goole Shipbuilding and Repairing Company Ltd, Goole, (Yard No.389), for the Ministry of War Transport, (Coastal Tankers Ltd, managers). 2.1943: Completed.   1946: Owners restyled as the Ministry of Transport, (Anglo-Saxon Petroleum Company Ltd, appointed as managers). 1947: Bulk Oil Steam Ship Company Ltd, appointed as chartering managers. 18.4.1947: Charter terminated and transferred to the Admiralty.   19.4.1947: Loaned to the Royal Hellenic Navy, Greece, and 1951 renamed POSEIDON. 1957: Renamed SIRIOS, to release the name for use on a submarine, newly purchased by the Royal Hellenic Navy on the 8th August 1957. 1962: Sold to the Royal Hellenic Navy. No further details.

CM.4. EMPIRE COPPICE (1943 - 1947)
O.N. 168764. 813g. 339n.   193.0 x 30.7 x 13.8 feet.   Tanker.
T.3-cyl. (15", 25½" & 41" x 30") 750 ihp engine manufactured by D. Rowan and Company Ltd, Glasgow.
27.3.1943: Launched by A. and J. Inglis Ltd., Glasgow, (Yard No.1190P), for the Ministry of War Transport, (Coastal Tankers Ltd, managers), London. 22.6.1943: Completed. 1945: Anglo-Saxon Petroleum Company Ltd, London, appointed as managers. 1946: Owners restyled the Ministry of Transport. 1947: Coastal Tankers Ltd, appointed as managers. 1947: Purchase procedures initiated by Coastal Tankers Ltd, (intended as ELKHOUND), but purchase was not concluded.   4.11.1947: Sold to the Kuwait Oil Company Ltd, London, and 1948 renamed AMIN. 1952: Sold to Shell-Mex and BP. Ltd, London, and renamed SHELL FITTER. 1964:

EMPIRE COPPICE as SHELL FITTER (WSPL)

Sold to Dionyssios I. Philippopoulos, Greece, and renamed ALIKI. 1967: Sold to Naftiki Adrotiki, (C. Vernicos, manager), Greece. 1968: Sold to Marine Water Supply Company Ltd, Greece. 10.9.1969: Kavership commenced demolition at Perama.

CM.5. TITUSVILLE (1943 - 1945)
O.N. 169589. 1,121g. 767n. 209.7 x 37.0 x 13.2 feet. Tanker.
5-cyl. 2 S.C.S.A. (405 x 505mm) 860 bhp, oil engine manufactured by Fairbanks, Morse and Company, Beloit, Wisconsin.
3.7.1942: Launched by the Barnes-Duluth Shipbuilding Company, Duluth, (Yard No.2), for the United States War Shipping Administration.
6.1943: Completed and bareboat chartered to the Ministry of War Transport, (Coastal Tankers Ltd, managers), London. 1945: Anglo-Saxon Petroleum Company Ltd, appointed managers. 1946: Charterers restyled the Ministry of Transport. 17.7.1946: Returned to the United States Maritime Commission. 1946: Sold to the China Merchants Steam Navigation Company, China, and renamed YUNG HAN (Tanker No.122). 1947: Transferred to the subsidiary, China Tanker Company Ltd, China. 24.5.1949: Scuttled in the Whangpo River during the Chinese hostilities.

CM.6. SPINDLETOP (1943 - 1945)
O.N. 169611. 1,155g. 697n. 213.7 x 37.1 x 14.3 feet. Tanker.
Post 1962: 938g. 496n. 213'6"x 37'0"x 14'6"
8-cyl. 4 S.C.S.A. (405 x 520mm) 860 bhp, oil engine manufactured by the Union Diesel Engine Company Oakland, California.
Post 1962: 12-cyl. 2 S.C.S.A. (8½" x 10") 1,200 bhp Vee type oil engine manufactured in 1960 by the General Motors Corporation, La Grange, Illinois.
12.12.1942: Launched by the Lancaster Ironworks Inc., Perryville, Maryland, (Yard No.201), for the United States War Shipping Administration. 8.1943: Completed and bareboat chartered to the Ministry of War Transport, (Coastal Tankers Ltd, managers), London. 1945: Anglo-Saxon Petroleum Company Ltd, appointed as managers. 1946: Charterer restyled the Ministry of Transport. 26.6.1946: Returned to

SPINDLETOP as LAKE CHARLES (WSPL)

the United States Maritime Commission. 1946: Sold to Lake Tankers Corporation, U.S.A., and renamed LAKE CHARLES. 1956/7: Owners restyled National Marine Service Inc., U.S.A. 1962: Sold to the United States Steel Corporation, and converted into a self - unloading cement carrier by the Southern Ship Building Corporation, Slidell, Louisiana, re-engined, and renamed ATLAS TRAVELLER, (operated by the Universal Atlas Cement Division). 1976: Sold to the Erie Navigation Company, U.S.A., and renamed LOC BAY. 1980: Sold to the Cement Transit Company, U.S.A., and renamed BADGER STATE. 1989: Demolished.

CM.7. CROMWELL (1943 - 1945)

O.N. 169659. 1,124g. 748n. 209.7 x 37.6 x 13.2 feet. Tanker.
5-cyl. 2 S.C.S.A. (405 x 505mm) 860 bhp, oil engine manufactured by Fairbanks, Morse and Company, Beloit, Wisconsin.
26.8.1942: Launched by the Barnes-Duluth Shipbuilding Company, Duluth, (Yard No.8), for the United States War Shipping Administration. 9.1943: Completed and bareboat chartered to the Ministry of War Transport, (Coastal Tankers Ltd., managers), London. 1945: Anglo-Saxon Petroleum Company Ltd, appointed as managers. 1946: Charterer restyled the Ministry of Transport. 12.6.1946: Returned to the United States Maritime Commission. 1946: Sold to the China Merchants Steam Navigation Company, China, and renamed YUNG CHANG (Tanker No.128). 1947: Transferred to the subsidiary, China Tanker Company Ltd, China. 1949: Sailed to Formosa, and reverted to the ownership of the parent company, China Merchants Steam Navigation Company, Formosa. 9.1963: Demolition commenced at Formosa.

CM.8. ROUSEVILLE (1943 - 1944)

O.N. 169728. 1,155g. 697n. 213.7 x 37.1 x 14.3 feet. Tanker.
8-cyl. 4 S.C.S.A. (405x 520mm) 860 bhp, oil engine manufactured by the Union Diesel Engine Company, Oakland, California.
4.7.1943: Launched by the Lancaster Iron Works Inc., Perryville, Maryland, (Yard No.203), for the United States War Shipping Administration. 10.1943: Completed and bareboat chartered to the Ministry of War Transport, (Coastal Tankers Ltd, managers). 26.10.1944: During a ballast voyage from Rouen to Le Havre, exploded a mine in the vicinity of Couerval Lighthouse, off Vieux Point, on the River Seine at a position 49.25N., 00.36E. The result started a fire in No.1 tank.

31.10.1944: Vessel was beached at Tancarville. Subsequently a petrol-gas explosion caused further damage to the vessel, breaking her back in two places. 1.11.1944: Vessel was reported abandoned as a total loss. The ultimate fate of the wreck is not recorded in official sources.

CM.9. CHANT 52 (1944 - 1946)
O.N. 169127. 401g. 211n. 141.7 x 27.1 x 8.5 feet.   Tanker.
4-cyl. 2 S.C.S.A. (10½" x 13½") 220 bhp, 4HRL type oil engine manufactured by Crossley Bros. Ltd, Manchester.
29.12.1943: Launched by Furness Shipbuilding Company Ltd, Haverton Hill-on-Tees, (Yard No.365), for the Ministry of War Transport, (Coastal Tankers Ltd, managers), London. 2.1944: Completed. 7.5.1946: Sold to T.B. McEwen and resold to Cia. de Nav. Lucia S.A., (P. Regazzoni, manager), Panama, and renamed LUCIA 2.   1948: Sold to Cominpex S.r.L., Italy. 1949: Sold to "Cofra" S.r.L., Italy. 1954: Sold to Giuseppe Colocotronis di Giovanni, Italy.   c1956: Official sources believe demolished.

CM.10. CHANT 53 (1944 - 1946)
O.N. 169128. 401g. 211n. 141.7 x 27.1 x 8.5 feet.   Tanker.
As built: 4-cyl. 2 S.C.S.A. (10½" x 13½") 220 bhp, 4HRL type oil engine manufactured by Crossley Bros. Ltd, Manchester.
Post 1964: 6-cyl. 2 S.C.S.A. (240 x 345mm) 220 bhp oil engine manufactured in 1950, by the Newbury Diesel Company Ltd, Newbury.
10.1.1944: Launched by Furness Shipbuilding Company Ltd, Haverton Hill-on-Tees, (Yard No.366), for the Ministry of War Transport, (Coastal Tankers Ltd, managers), London. 2.1944: Completed. 26.4.1946: Sold to Geo. Fokias and resold to the Royal Netherlands Government, (N.V. Teer Bedrijf Uithoorn, managers), Holland, and renamed THEODORA. 1950: Sold to N.V. Rederij "Theodora", Holland. 1954: Sold to F.T. Everard and Sons Ltd, London, and renamed AVERITY. 1964: Re-engined. 23.6.1972: West of Scotland Shipbreaking Company Ltd, commenced demolition at Troon.

AVERITY, ex CHANT 53   *(WSPL)*

CM.11. CHANT 54 (1944 - 1946)

O.N. 169129. 401g. 211n. 141.7 x 27.1 x 8.5 feet.   Tanker.
6-cyl. 2 S.C.S.A. (180 x 300mm) 240 bhp M46E Polar type oil engine
manufactured by British Auxiliaries Ltd, Glasgow.
24.1.1944: Launched by the Furness Shipbuilding Company Ltd,
Haverton Hill-on-Tees, (Yard No.367), for the Ministry of War Transport,
(Coastal Tankers Ltd, managers). 1944: Completed. 1946: Owners
restyled the Ministry of Transport. 10.7.1946: Sold to A/S Ryvarden, (F.N.
Nordbö, manager), Norway, and renamed STEINSFJELL. 1946: Sold to
the Union Steamship Company of South Africa Ltd, Cape Town, and
renamed GENERAL MITCHELL BAKER. 1947: Converted into a dry
cargoship, and renamed KLAVER. 1949: Renamed BECHUANA (Coast
Lines Africa (Pty) Ltd, managers). 11.12.1950: Whilst on a voyage from
Port Nolloth to Cape Town with 3,000 cartons of canned Crayfish,
stranded 30 miles South from Port Nolloth, Cape of Good Hope. 1951:
The Eastern Trading Company attempted salvage, but had to abandon
work due to worsening weather.

CM.12. CHANT 55 (1944 - 1946)

O.N. 169130. 401g. 211n. 141.7 x 27.1 x 8.5 feet.   Tanker.
6-cyl. 2 S.C.S.A. (180 x 300mm) 240 bhp M46E Polar type oil engine
manufactured by British Auxiliaries Ltd, Glasgow.
31.1.1944: Launched by the Furness Shipbuilding Company Ltd,
Haverton Hill-on-Tees, (Yard No.368), for the Ministry of War Transport,
(Coastal Tankers Ltd, managers). 3.1944: Completed. 1946: Owners
restyled the Ministry of Transport. 14.5.1946: Sold to Raymond K.
Makzoume, Syria. 1947: Sold to M.H. Kodsi, Syria, and renamed ABDUL
KADER. 1948: Sold to Toufic Battache, Lebanon, and renamed TONY.
1954: Sold to Levant Shipping Company, (S.A.L.), Lebanon, and
converted into a dry cargo vessel. 1956: Sold to Antoniou and Giliates,
Greece, and renamed MARIA. 1962: Sold to S. Kontos, D. Gioldassis and
Company, Greece. 3.9.1966: Whilst on a voyage from Haifa to
Famagusta, with cement, she developed leaks and was abandoned by
her crew, subsequently sinking at a position 34.21N., 35.05E., off the
southern coast of Cyprus.

CM.13. CHANT 56 (1944 - 1946)

O.N. 169131. 392g. 160n. 141.7 x 27.1 x 8.5 feet.   Tanker.
6-cyl. 2 S.C.S.A. (180 x 300mm) 240 bhp M46E Polar type oil engine
manufactured by British Auxiliaries Ltd, Glasgow.
10.2.1944: Launched by the Furness Shipbuilding Company Ltd,
Haverton Hill-on-Tees, (Yard No.369), for the Ministry of War Transport,
(Coastal Tankers Ltd, managers). 3.1944: Completed. 1946: Owners
restyled the Ministry of Transport, (F.T. Everard and Sons Ltd, appointed
as managers). 4.10.1946: Sold to Anglo-Saxon Petroleum Company Ltd,
London. 1947: Resold to N.V. Nederlandsche-Indische Tank Stoomboot
Maatschappij, Holland, and renamed MILO. 1949: Owners restyled N.V.
Nederlands-Indonesische Tankvaart Maatschappij. 1956: Sold to N.V.
Petroleum Maatschappij "La Corona", (Shell Tankers N.V., managers),
Holland. 25.5.1958: Sold to the Military Authority of Palembang, with the
proviso that the vessel would be demolished. 26.3.1960: The last report
of vessel was that she was in a poor condition but demolition had not
yet commenced.

CM.14. CHANT 57 (1944 - 1946)

O.N. 169133. 409g. 169n. 141.7 x 27.1 x 8.5 feet.   Tanker.
As built: 6-cyl. 2 S.C.S.A. (180 x 300mm) 240 bhp M46E Polar type oil engine manufactured by British Auxiliaries Ltd, Glasgow.
Post 1953: 5-cyl. 2 S.C.S.A. (240 x 400mm) 300 bhp B. and W. type oil engine manufactured by Frederikshavns Jernst and Maskinfabrik, Frederikshavn.
11.2.1944: Launched by the Furness Shipbuilding Company Ltd, Haverton Hill-on-Tees, (Yard No.370), for the Ministry of War Transport, (Coastal Tankers Ltd, managers). 4.1944: Completed. 1946: Owners restyled the Ministry of Transport, (F.T. Everard and Sons Ltd, appointed as managers). 18.4.1946: Sold to Rethymnis and Kulukundis Ltd, Greece, and renamed GRANDE and resold to Rederi A/B. Staffan, (J. Haag, manager), Sweden, and renamed GRAN. 1953: Re-engined. 1966: Sold to Stockholms Rederi A/B Svea, Sweden, and resold to the Maritime Company Ltd, Iran, and renamed KAMRAN. 18.1.1989: Whilst on a voyage from Dubai to Iran, foundered in heavy weather off Abu Musa, United Arab Emirates, at position 25.50N., 55.22E.

CHANT 58 as built   *(WSPL)*

CM.15. CHANT 58 (1944 - 1946)

O.N. 169134. 401g. 171n. 141.7 x 27.1 x 8.2 feet.   Tanker.
As built: 6-cyl. 2 S.C.S.A. (180 x 300mm) 240 bhp M46E Polar type oil engine manufactured by British Auxiliaries Ltd, Glasgow.
Post 1958: 4-cyl. 2 S.C.S.A. (10$\frac{1}{2}$" x 13$\frac{1}{2}$") 380 bhp oil engine manufactured by Crossley Bros. Ltd, Manchester.
23.2.1944: Launched by the Furness Shipbuilding Company Ltd, Haverton Hill-on-Tees, (Yard No.371), for the Ministry of War Transport, (Coastal Tankers Ltd, managers). 4.1944: Completed. 1946: Owners restyled the Ministry of Transport. 16.7.1946: Sold to Booker Brothers, McConnell and Company Ltd, British Guiana, and renamed KAMUNI. 9.1946: Converted to a dry cargo vessel. 1950: Owners restyled Bookers Shipping (Demerara) Ltd. 6.1958: Re-engined. 1989: Lloyd's Register removed entry as continued existence was in doubt.

CM.16. CHANT 59 (1944 - 1946)

O.N. 169135. 395g. 182n. 140.9 x 27.0 x 8.3 feet. Tanker.
6-cyl. 2 S.C.S.A. (180 x 300mm) 240 bhp M46E Polar type oil engine manufactured by British Auxiliaries Ltd, Glasgow.
29.2.1944: Launched by the Furness Shipbuilding Company Ltd, Haverton Hill-on-Tees, (Yard No.372), for the Ministry of War Transport, (Coastal Tankers Ltd, managers). 4.1944: Completed. 1946: Owners restyled as the Ministry of Transport. 11.7.1946: Sold to Rederi Ab Havnia, (Algot Johansson, manager), Finland, and renamed HELNY. 1954: Sold to the Naval Agency Corp. S.A., Costa Rica, and renamed MARIA ROSA. 1958: Sold to Marine Tankers S.A., Panama. 11.9.1965: Francisco Alberich commenced demolition at Barcelona, and completed work on 8.10.1965.

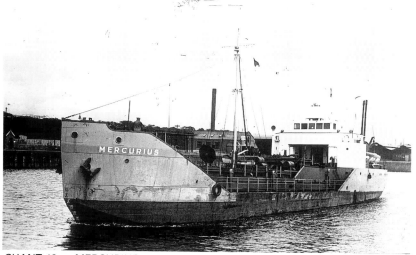

CHANT 42 as MERCURIUS   (WSPL)

CM.17. CHANT 42 (1944 - 1946)

O.N. 169141. 400g. 215n. 141.8 x 27.1 x 8.5 feet. Tanker.
As built: 6-cyl. 4 S.C.S.A. (215 x 350mm) 270 bhp, TLR6 type oil engine manufactured by Mirrlees, Bickerton and Day Ltd, Stockport.
Post 1954: 6-cyl. 4 S.C.S.A. (290 x 420mm) 390 bhp oil engine manufactured in 1953, by Maschinenfabrik Kiel A.G., Kiel.
9.5.1944: Launched by the Furness Shipbuilding Company Ltd, Haverton Hill-on-Tees, (Yard No.383), for the Ministry of War Transport, (Coastal Tankers Ltd, managers). 6.1944: Completed. 1946: Owners restyled the Ministry of Transport. 8.7.1946: Sold to A/S Ryvarden, (F.N. Nordbö, manager), Norway, and renamed RAMSFJELL. 1947: Sold to Amsterdamsche Scheepvaart Bedrijf C.V., Holland, and renamed MERCURIUS. 1954: Re-engined. 1956: Sold to N.V. Amsterdamsche Rederi Tot Exploitatie van Het M.T.S. Mercurius, Holland. 1961: Sold to Visgroothandel Fa Joh Kuyten, Holland, and converted into a live fish carrier. 7.1968: Laid up with surveys overdue. 1972: Sold to Scheepvaarts en Handelges Hujo A.G., Holland. 5.1974: Demolition commenced at New Lekkerland, Holland..

CM.18. CHANT 43 (1944 - 1946)

O.N. 169142. 401g. 212n. 141.7 x 27.1 x 8.5 feet. Tanker.
6-cyl. 4 S.C.S.A. (215 x 350mm) 270 bhp, TLR6 type oil engine manufactured by Mirrlees, Bickerton and Day Ltd, Stockport.
10.5.1944: Launched by the Furness Shipbuilding Company Ltd, Haverton Hill-on-Tees, (Yard No.384), for the Ministry of War Transport, (Coastal Tankers Ltd, managers). 6.1944: Completed. 1946: Owners restyled as the Ministry of Transport. 30.9.1946: Sold to the Anglo-Saxon Petroleum Company Ltd, London, and 1947 renamed RUSA. 1947: Transferred to Shell Company of Straits Settlements Ltd, London. 1949: Owners restyled as Shell Company of Singapore Ltd, London. 1958: Sold to Tiong Lam Hang Ltd, Singapore, but retaining her London registry. 1959: Sold to Tan Kim Heng, Singapore. 1962: Sold to Tiong Lam Hang Shipping Company S.A., Panama. 1986: Name deleted from registers - continued existence in doubt.

CM.19. CHANT 44 (1944 - 1946)

O.N. 169144. 401g. 212n. 141.7 x 27.1 x 8.5 feet. Tanker.
As built: 6-cyl. 4 S.C.S.A. (215 x 350mm) 270 bhp, TLR6 type oil engine manufactured by Mirrlees, Bickerton and Day Ltd, Stockport.
Post 1951: 5-cyl. 2 S.C.S.A. (250 x 420mm) Polar type oil engine manufactured by British Polar Engines Ltd, Glasgow.
24.5.1944: Launched by the Furness Shipbuilding Company Ltd, Haverton Hill-on-Tees, (Yard No.385), for the Ministry of War Transport, (Coastal Tankers Ltd. managers). 6.1944: Completed. 1946: Owners restyled the Ministry of Transport. 27.7.1946: Sold to Constantine E. Vlassopoulos, Panama, converted into a dry cargo vessel, and renamed

MASHONA COAST, ex CHANT 44, converted from tanker to dry cargo ship
(WSPL)

ANDRONIKI. 1947: Sold to the Union Steamship Company of South Africa Ltd., and renamed OKIEP. 1949: Renamed MASHONA, (Coast Lines Africa (Pty) Ltd, appointed as managers). 1951: Re-engined. 1953: Renamed MASHONA COAST, (Thesens Steamship Company Ltd, managers). 1964: Engine removed whilst vessel was adapted for use as a storage hulk. 3.1965: Sold to the Marine Diamond Corporation Ltd, Cape Town, converted into a dumb barge. No further details known.

CM.20. CHANT 45 (1944 - 1946)

O.N. 169145. 401g. 212n. 141.7 x 27.1 x 8.5 feet. Tanker.
As built: 6-cyl. 4 S.C.S.A. (215 x 350mm) 270 bhp, TLR6 type oil engine manufactured by Mirrlees, Bickerton and Day Ltd, Stockport.
Post 1958: 6-cyl. 4 S.C.S.A. (265 x 410mm) 375 bhp oil engine manufactured by Ansaldo Stab Mecc., Genoa.
25.5.1944: Launched by the Furness Shipbuilding Company Ltd, Haverton Hill-on-Tees, (Yard No.386), for the Ministry of War Transport, (Coastal Tankers Ltd, managers). 6.1944: Completed. 1946: Owners restyled the Ministry of Transport. 25.7.1946: Sold to J.N. Vassiliou, Panama. 1947: Sold to Constatine Machairas, Panama, and renamed MARO. 1948: Sold to Les Cargos Fruitiers Chérifiens Société Anonime, Morocco, and renamed SEID. 1951: Sold to Société Maritime de Transports Oceano - Mediterraneens (SOMATROM), (Mérigot et Compagnie, managers), Morocco, converted into a wine tanker, and renamed SAINTE FRANÇOISE II. 1955: Sold to E. Mérigot et Compagnie, Algiers. 1958: Re-engined. 1962: Sold to Leone Bianchi and Figlio, Italy, and renamed NAPOLEONE PRIMO. 1974: Name deleted from registers as believed converted into a non-propelled barge.

CM.21. EMPIRE JURA (1944)

O.N. 169419. 813g. 334n. 193.0 x 30.7 x 13.8 feet. Tanker.
T.3-cyl. (15", 25½" & 41" x 30") 750 ihp engine manufactured by D. Rowan and Company Ltd, Glasgow.
28.8.1944: Launched by A. and J. Inglis Ltd, Glasgow, (Yard No.1282P), for the Ministry of War Transport, (Coastal Tankers Ltd, designated as managers), London. 16.10.1944: Completed, Anglo-Saxon Petroleum Company Ltd, appointed as managers. 1946: Owners restyled the Ministry of Transport, (Coastal Tankers Ltd, appointed as managers). 7.2.1946: Sold to Van Castricum and Company Ltd, London, and renamed SAMSHOO. 1947: Sold to Samshoo Tanker Company Ltd, (E. Gray and Company, managers), London. 1951: Sold to Bulk Oil Steam Ship Company Ltd, London, and renamed PASS OF GLENOGLE. 1961: Sold to Augusto Garolla and Company, Italy, and renamed MARCELLO GAROLLA. 1970: Sold to Sarda Bunkers S.p.A., Italy, and renamed MARCELLO G. 19.2.1972: Whilst undergoing repairs at Naples developed a list in heavy weather, heeled over and sank. 2.8.1972: Raised and although declared a constructive total loss was in fact repaired and returned to service by her owners. 21.3.1979: Messers Montagna commenced demolition at Naples.

CM.22. EMPIRE BUTE (1944 - 1945)

O.N. 169424. 813g. 334n. 193.0 x 30.7 x 13.8 feet. Tanker.
T.3-cyl. (15", 25½" & 41" x 30") 750 ihp engine manufactured by Aitchison, Blair Ltd, Clydebank.
19.10.1944: Launched by A. and J Inglis Ltd., Glasgow, (Yard No.1286P), for the Ministry of War Transport, (Coastal Tankers Ltd, managers). 22.12.1944: Completed. 1945: Anglo-Saxon Petroleum Co. Ltd, appointed as managers. 11.4.l946: Owners restyled as the Ministry of Transport. 1946: Sold to Société Algèrriene de Navigation Pour L'Afrique du Nord, (Ch. Schiaffino and Compagnie, managers), Algeria, and renamed MILIANA. 1948: Sold to Scotto, Ambrosino Pugliese Fils et Compagnie, Algeria, and renamed RIVOLI. 1952: Sold to Bulk Oil Steam Ship Company Ltd, London, and renamed PASS OF DRUMOCHTER. 1962: Sold to Lugari and Filippi, Italy, and renamed SANTA GUILIA. 1970: Sold to Chimigas S.p.A., Italy. 1971: Sold to "Ciane Anapo" Compania di

EMPIRE BUTE as PASS OF DRUMOCHTER (WSPL)

Nav. e Bunkeraggi S.p.A., Italy. 1971: Sold to Fratelli Novella, Genoa. 1971: Demolished by Ditta Lotti at La Spezia.

CM.23. DARST CREEK (1944 - 1945)
O.N. 169842. 1,135g. 686n. 213.8 x 37.1 x 14.3 feet. Tanker. 8-cyl. 4 S.C.S.A. (370 x 505mm) 814 bhp, oil engine manufactured by the National Supply Corporation, Springfield, Mass.
30.5.1943: Launched by Gray's Iron Works Inc., Galveston, (Yard No.105), for the United States War Shipping Administration. 6.1943: Completed. 1.2.1944: Bareboat chartered to the Ministry of War Transport, (Coastal Tankers Ltd, managers), London. 1945: Anglo-Saxon Petroleum Company Ltd, appointed as managers. 1946: Charterer restyled as the Ministry of Transport. 13.8.1946: Returned to the United States Maritime Commission. 1946: Sold to China Merchants Steam Navigation Company, China, and renamed YUNG HUANG (Tanker No.103). 1947:

DARST CREEK (WSPL)

98

Transferred to the subsidiary, China Tanker Company Ltd, China,. 1949: Taken over by the Government of the People's Republic of China, and later registered in the ownership of the China Ocean Shipping Company. (C.O.S.C.O.). 11.1991: Lloyd's Register removed entry as continued existence was in doubt.

CM.24. HASTINGS (1944 - 1945)

O.N. 169869. 1,135g. 686n. 213.8 x 37.0 x 14.3 feet. Tanker.
8-cyl. 4 S.C.S.A. (405 x 505mm) 814 bhp, oil engine manufactured by the Union Diesel Engine Company, Oakland, California.
30.10.1943: Launched by Todd Galveston Dry Dock Inc., Shipbuilding Division (formerly Gray's Ironworks Inc.), Galveston, (Yard No.108), for the United States War Shipping Administration. 4.1944: Completed and bareboat chartered to the Ministry of War Transport, (Coastal Tankers Ltd, managers), London. 1945: Anglo-Saxon Petroleum Company Ltd, London, appointed as managers. 1946: Charterer restyled the Ministry of Transport. 20.8.1946: Returned to the United States Maritime Commission. 1946: Sold to the China Merchants Steam Navigation Company, Kaohsiung, and renamed YUNG LAI (Tanker No.101). 1947: Transferred to the subsidiary, China Tanker Company Ltd, China. 1949: Sailed to Formosa, and reverted to the parent company, China Merchants Steam Navigation Company, Formosa. 9.1966: Demolished at Formosa.

EMPIRE TADPOLE   *(WSPL)*

CM.25. EMPIRE TADPOLE (1944 - 1947)

O.N. 123965. 1,798g. 1,148n. 250 x 42.7 x 17.4 feet. Tanker.
Post 1940: 1,752g. 1,029n.
As built: T.3-cyl. (17", 28" & 46" x 33") 121 nhp engine manufactured by the North Eastern Marine Engineering Company Ltd, Sunderland.
Post 1940: 6-cyl. 2S.C.S.A. (405 x 510mm) 1,050 bhp oil engine manufactured by Fairbanks, Morse and Compny, Beloit.
Post 1961: 6-cyl. 2S.C.S.A. (405 x 510mm) 1,050 bhp oil engine manufactured by Fairbanks, Morse and Company, Beloit.
25.2.1910: Launched by the Sunderland Shipbuilding Company Ltd, Sunderland, (Yard No.256), as the general cargoship SASKATOON, for the the Merchants Mutual Line, (J.W. Norcross, manager), Montreal, the vessel being registered at Sunderland. 4.1910: Completed. 1914: Owners restyled as Merchants Mutual Lakes Line Ltd, (J.W. Norcross, manager). 1915: Canada Steamship Company, appointed as managers. 1916: Sold to Canadian Northern Steamship Ltd, Canada. 1918: Sold to the Canadian Maritime Company Ltd, Canada. 1919: Sold to E.J. Heinz

(London) Ltd, and the vessel re-registered at Montreal. 1922: Sold to the Interlake Navigation Company Ltd, Montreal. 1926: Sold to the Canada Steamship Lines Ltd, Montreal, and renamed ROSEMOUNT. 24.11.1934: Sank alongside Century Coal Dock, Montreal. 25.5.1935: Raised and subsequently declared a "constructive total loss", sold to Manseau Shipyards Ltd, (J.E. Simard, manager), Montreal, partially dismantled and transferred to Manseau Shipping Ltd, (same manager), Montreal and used as a floating grain store. 1937: Removed from the Register books. 1940: Converted into the motor tanker WILLOWBRANCH and registered under Branch Lines Ltd, (Marine Industries Ltd, managers), Sorel. 1.12.1944: Sold to the Ministry of War Transport, (Coastal Tankers Ltd, managers), London, and renamed EMPIRE TADPOLE. 1946: Owners restyled the Ministry of Transport. 1.1947: Sold to the Bulk Storage Company Ltd, (P. Bauer, manager), London, who later restyled as Basinghall Shipping Company Ltd, (same managers), London, and renamed BASINGCREEK. 1950: Sold to Canadian Sealakers Ltd, (Transit Tankers and Terminals Ltd, managers), Canada, and renamed COASTAL CREEK. 1961: Re-engined with identical machinery. 1968: Sold to Hall Corporation of Canada Shipping (1968) Ltd, Canada, and renamed CREEK TRANSPORT. 1972: Sold to R.L. Fisher, Montreal. 1972: Sold to the Richelieu Dredging Corporation Inc., McNamara Corporation Ltd, and J.P. Porter Company Ltd, Canada, and renamed ILE DE MONTREAL. 1976: Sold to the Nittolo Metal Company Inc., Canada. 1987: Demolished.

CM.26. RIDING MOUNTAIN PARK / EMPIRE PIKE (1944 - 1946)

O.N. 134184. 1,605g. 887n.   245.0 x 42.8 x 18.0 feet.   Tanker.
Post 1943:   1,854g. 887n.   240.2 x 42.8 x 18.0 feet.
Two, T.3-cyl. (14", 22" & 36" x 21") engines manufactured by Polson Ironworks, Toronto, connected to twin propeller shafts.
1905: Completed by the Government Shipyard, Sorel, Quebec, as the dredger, W.S.FIELDING, for the Canadian Government. 1914: Renamed P.W.D. No.I., for the Minister of Public Works for Canada. 1943: Converted into a tanker, by the St John's Dry Dock and Shipbuilding Company for the Government of the Dominion of Canada, and renamed RIDING MOUNTAIN PARK, (Park Steamship Company, managers), Canada. 10.11.1944: Purchased by the Ministry of War Transport, (Coastal Tankers Ltd, managers), London, and 1945 renamed EMPIRE PIKE. 1946: Owners restyled as the Ministry of Transport. 28.11.1946: Sold to the Bulk Storage Company Ltd, London, (P. Bauer, manager), who later restyled as Basinghall Shipping Company Ltd, London, (same managers), and renamed BASINGFORD. 1948: Management terminated. 1949: Sold to the British Iron and Steel Corporation (Salvage) Ltd, and allocated to Clayton and Davie Ltd, Dunston-on-Tyne for demolition. 29.10.1949: Work commenced.

CM.27. EMPIRE TIGONTO (1945) and (1945 - 1946)

O.N. 180734.   664g. 332n.   192.5 x 29.7 x 12.4 feet.   Tanker.
Two, 6-cyl.   4 S.C.S.A. oil engines manufactured by Motorenwerke Mannheim A.G., Mannheim. 900 bhp.
1938: Ordered from D.W. Kremer Sohn, Elmshorn, (Yard No.853), by the Kriegsmarine. 25.4.1941: Completed as DORA for the Luftwaffe, for employment in the Baltic and North Seas. 1945: Taken by the Allied Authorities at Flensburg and allocated to the Ministry of War Transport (Coastal Tankers Ltd, managers), and renamed EMPIRE TIGONTO. 1945:

Anglo-Saxon Petroleum Company Ltd, appointed as managers 1945: Coastal Tankers Ltd, re-appointed as managers. 1946: Owners restyled the Ministry of Transport. 27.5.1946: Sold to the Government of Russia. 1959: Lloyd's Register deleted the entry due to the lack of information.

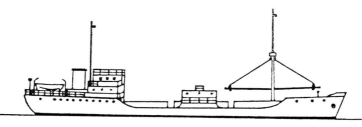

Seetankschiff *Anna* (Klasse T I) (Grö)

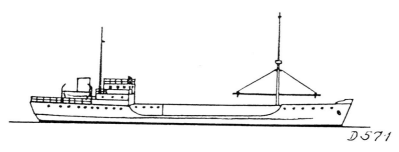

Seetankschiff *Dora. Else. Grete. Hanna*

CM.28. EMPIRE TIGOUVER (1945) and (1945 - 1946)

O.N. 180735. 664g. 332n. 192.5 x 29.7 x 12.4 feet. Tanker.
Two, 6-cyl. 4 S.C.S.A. oil engines manufactured by Motorenwerke Mannheim A.G., Mannheim.
1938: Ordered from D.W. Kremer Sohn, Elmshorn, (Yard No.858), by the Kriegsmarine. 22.5.1943: Completed as GRETE for the Luftwaffe for employment in the Baltic and North Seas. 1945: Taken by the Allied Authorities, and allocated to the Ministry of War Transport, London., (Coastal Tankers Ltd, managers), and renamed EMPIRE TIGOUVER. 1945: Anglo-Saxon Petroleum Company Ltd, appointed as managers 1945: Coastal Tankers Ltd, re-appointed as managers. 1946: Owners restyled the Ministry of Transport. 27.5.1946: Sold to the Government of Russia and 23.6.1946: Arrived at Swinemunde. 1959: Lloyd's Register deleted the entry due to the lack of information.

CM.29. EMPIRE TIGINA (1945 - 1946)

O.N. 180736. 638g. 320n. 189.4 x 29.6 x 12.4 feet. Tanker.
Two, 6-cyl. 4 S.C.S.A. oil engines manufactured by Motorenwerke Mannheim A.G., Mannheim.
1938: Ordered from D.W. Kremer Sohn, Elmshorn, (Yard No.854), by the

Kriegsmarine. 25.7.1941: Completed as ELSE for the Luftwaffe, for employment in the Baltic and North Seas. 1945: Taken by the Allied Authorities, and allocated to the Ministry of War Transport, (Coastal Tankers Ltd, managers) and renamed EMPIRE TIGINA. 1946: Owners restyled the Ministry of Transport. 30.9.1945: Arrived at Burntisland. 19.6.1946: Sold to the Government of Russia and 21.6.1946: Arrived at Swinemunde. 1959: Lloyd's Register deleted the entry due to the lack of information.

CM.30. EMPIRE TEGYIKA (1945 - 1947)
O.N. 180797. 1,593g. 737n.   244.1 x 41.4 x 16.9 feet.   Tanker.
As built: Two, 6-cyl. 4 S.C.S.A. (365 x 500mm) MAN type oil engines manufactured by Maschinenfabrik Augsburg-Nurnberg A.G., Augsburg, geared to twin screw shafts. 1,200 bhp.
Post 1958: Two, 8-cyl. 4 S.C.S.A. (220 x 292mm) 660 bhp, ERSMGR8 type oil engines manufactured by Lister, Blackstone Marine Ltd, Dursley.
4.1935: Completed by H.C. Stulcken Sohn, Hamburg, (Yard No.695), as LISELOTTE ESSBERGER for Atlantic Tank Reederei G.m.b.H., (John T. Essberger G.m.b.H., managers), Hamburg. 1937: Sold to John T. Essberger G.m.b.H., Hamburg. 5.1945: Seized by the Allied Authorities at Trondheim and allocated to the Ministry of War Transport, (Anglo-Saxon Petroleum Company Ltd, managers) and renamed EMPIRE

CAROLINE M, ex EMPIRE TEGYIKA   (WSPL)

TEGYIKA. 1945: Coastal Tankers Ltd, appointed as managers. 1946: Owners restyled the Ministry of Transport. 31.1.1947: Transferred to the Admiralty, and renamed THORNOL. 1948: Sold to Metcalf Motor Coasters Ltd, (Thomas J. Metcalf, manager), London, and renamed CAROLINE M. 1958: Re-engined. 1966: Sold to the Greek Tankershipping Company Ltd, Piraeus, and renamed KYLLINI.   12.1980: Salimis S.A., commenced demolition, at Salimis Island.

CM.31. ANNA (1945 - 1946)
638g. 320n.   189.4 x 29.6 x 12.4 feet.   Tanker.
Two 6-cyl. 4 S.C.S.A. oil engines manufactured by Motorenwerke Mannheim A.G., Mannheim.

1938: Ordered from D.W. Kremer Sohn, Elmshorn, (Yard No.836), by the Kriegsmarine. 6.4.1940: Completed as ANNA for the Luftwaffe, (Atlantic Reederei, managers), for employment in the Baltic and North Seas. 5.1945: Seized by the Allied Authorities at Kristiansand, Norway, and allocated to the Ministry of War Transport, (Coastal Tankers Ltd, managers), London. 14.9.1945: Arrived at Burntisland, to have been renamed EMPIRE TIGAWA, but was returned to Norway to act as a supply ship for German Minesweeping Administration. 27.12.1945: As British flag ANNA, (no O.N. located), stranded at Bolsax, Kattegat and was badly damaged. Subsequently refloated and taken to Kalundborg, Denmark. 11.1946: Vessel was reported as based at Cuxhaven. 9.1947: Transferred to France and renamed L'ARDECHE. No further details.

CM.32. HILDE (1945 - 1946)
638g. 320n. 189.4 x 29.6 x 12.4 feet. Tanker.
Two 6-cyl. 4 S.C.S.A. oil engines manufactured by Motorenwerke Mannheim A.G., Mannheim.
1938: Ordered from D.W. Kremer Sohn, Elmshorn, (Yard No.859), by the Kriegsmarine. 22.9.1943: Completed as HANNA for the Luftwaffe, for employment in the Baltic and North Seas. 1.12.1944: Renamed HILDE, (to avoid confusion with her sistership ANNA see CM.31). 5.1945: Seized by the Allied Authorities at Kristiansand, Norway, and allocated to the Ministry of War Transport, (Coastal Tankers Ltd, managers), and to have been renamed EMPIRE TIGOSTI. 1946: Owners restyled the Ministry of Transport. 19.6.1946: Re-allocated to Russia as HILDE. 20.6.1946: Arrived at Swinemunde. No further trace.

CM.33. CHANT 26 (1945)
O.N. 180111. 388g. 125n. 142.1 x 27.1 x 8.4 feet. Tanker.
As built: 4-cyl. 2S.C.S.A. ($10\frac{1}{2}$" x $13\frac{1}{2}$") 220 bhp, 4HRL type oil engine manufactured by Crossley Bros.Ltd, Manchester.
Post 1958: 5-cyl. 2S.C.S.A. (250 x 420mm) 325 bhp oil engine manufactured by Nydqvist and Holm A/B., Trollhattan.
28.3.1944: Launched by the Goole Shipbuilding and Repairing Company Ltd, Goole, (Yard No.414), for the Ministry of War Transport, (F.T. Everard and Sons Ltd, managers). 4.1944: Completed. 8.1945: Coastal Tankers Ltd, appointed as managers. 22.8.1945: Transferred to the Admiralty and removed from management. 25.6.1946: Sold to Beaconray Steam Ship Co.Ltd, and resold to Finska Angfartygs A/B., Finland, and renamed T.1. 1951: Sold to Reuters Handels A/B., (Hakon Reuter, manager), Sweden, and renamed B.T. IX. 6.1958: Re-engined, and renamed SVARTSKAR. 1959: Sold to A/B Bensintransport, (Gosta Reuter, manager), Sweden, and renamed B.T. IX. 1963: Sold to F. Visentini, Italy, and renamed FOCA. 1967: Sold to Angelo Hopps, Italy. 1969: Sold to Foca-Miriam S.r.L., Italy. 10.1974: Sold for demolition at Spezia.

CM.34. CHANT 28 (1945)
O.N. 180115. 402g. 215n. 142.2 x 27.0 x 8.5 feet. Tanker.
7-cyl. 4 S.C.S.A. (220 x 290mm) oil engine manufactured by R.A. Lister (Marine Sales) Ltd, Dursley.
20.5.1944: Launched by the Goole Shipbuilding and Repairing Company Ltd, Goole, (Yard No.416), for the Ministry of War Transport, (F.T. Everard and Sons Ltd, managers). 5.1944: Completed. 11.1945: Coastal Tankers Ltd, appointed as managers. 1.12.1945: Sold to Port Autonome du Havre, France. 1986: Sold to Fablon et Compagnie, for demolition at Le Havre.

CM.35. EMPIRE JEWEL **(1946)** see ship No. HM.10.

CM.36. EMPIRE TEGAYA (1946)
O.N. 180648. 2,770g. 1,517n.　309.7 x 45.5 x 22.5 feet.　　　Tanker.
Post 1934:　3,145g. 343.4 x 45.5 x 22.5 feet.
6-cyl. 4S.C.S.A. (630 x 960mm) 1,200 bhp oil engine by Algemeine Electric Ges., Berlin.
29.10.1921: Launched by Deutsche Werft A.G., Hamburg, (Yard No.45), as JULIUS SCHINDLER for Oelwerke Julius Schindler G.m.b.H., Hamburg. 2.1922: Completed. 1925: Sold to Masconomo G.m.b.H., Hamburg. 1926: Sold to Tankschiffreederei Julius Schindler G.m.b.H., Hamburg. 1934: Lengthened. 1939: Sold to Hamburger Tank Reederei G.m.b.H., (Atlantic Reederei F. and W. Joch, managers), Hamburg, and renamed THALATTA. 5.1945: Seized by the Allied Authorities at Kiel, and allocated to the Ministry of War Transport, (Anglo-Saxon Petroleum Company Ltd, managers) and renamed EMPIRE TEGAYA. 1946: Coastal Tankers Ltd, appointed as managers,. 1946: Owners restyled as the Ministry of Transport, (Anglo-Saxon Petroleum Company Ltd, appointed as managers). 28.1.1947: Sold to the Haddon Steamship Company Ltd, London, and renamed ARTIST. 1947: Transferred to the Valiant Steamship Company Ltd, London. 1950: Sold to Fundador Compania Naviera S.A., Panama, and renamed ASTRO. 1953: Sold to the Nolido Compania de Naviera S.A., Panama, and renamed FRANCO LISI. 1956: Sold to the Ocean Trading Corporation, Panama. 1959: Sold to the Nolido Compania de Naviera S.A., Panama. 21.7.1959: Laid up at Syra. 19.11.1959: Arrived at La Spezia, for demolition but was resold, and 23.12.1959: Arrived at Savona for demolition, by Guiseppe Ricardi.

EMPIRE SHETLAND　　　　　　　　　　　　　　　　　　　　　　　(WSPL)

CM.37. EMPIRE BAIRN (1946/47 - 1948)

O.N. 168702. 813g. 333n. 193.0 x 30.7 x 13.8 feet. Tanker.
T.3-cyl. (15", 25½" & 41" x 30") 750 ihp engine manufactured by D. Rowan and Company Ltd, Glasgow.
23.10.1941: Launched by Blythswood Shipbuilding Company Ltd, Glasgow, (Yard No.67), for the Ministry of War Transport, (Bulk Oil Steam Ship Company Ltd, managers). 12.1941: Completed. 1945: Anglo-Saxon Petroleum Company Ltd, London, appointed as managers. 1946: Owners restyled as the Ministry of Transport. 1946/47: Coastal Tankers Ltd, appointed as managers. 17.3.1948: Sold to the Indian Navy, and renamed CHIKLA. 1975: In service as a yard-craft. 1977: Demolished.

CM.38. EMPIRE HARP (2) (1946 - 1948) see ship No. CM.2.

CM.39. THORNOL (1947 - 1948) see ship No. CM.30.

CM.40. EMPIRE SHETLAND (1947)

O.N. 169436. 813g. 334n. 193.0 x 30.7 x 13.8 feet. Tanker.
T.3-cyl. (15", 25½" & 41" x 30") 750 ihp engine manufactured by Rankin and Blackmore Ltd, Glasgow.
19.1.1945: Launched by A. and J. Inglis Ltd, Glasgow, (Yard No.1288P), for the Ministry of War Transport, (Anglo-Saxon Petroleum Company Ltd, managers). 11.4.1945: Completed. 1946: Owners restyled as the Ministry of Transport. 1947: Coastal Tankers Ltd, appointed as managers. 3.10.1947: Sold to the Kuwait Oil Company Ltd, (Anglo-Iranian Oil Company Ltd, managers), London, and renamed ADIB. 1952: Sold to Shell-Mex and B.P. Ltd, London, and renamed B.P. TRANSPORTER. 18.6.1965: Scrappingco S.A., Brussels, commenced demolition at Antwerp.

EMPIRE FITZROY *(WSPL)*

CM.41. EMPIRE FITZROY (1950 - 1952)

O.N. 169450. 890g. 379n. 193.0 x 32.0 x 14.5 feet. Tanker.
4-cyl. 2S.C.S.A. (335 x 570mm) 1,140 bhp oil engine manufactured by British Polar Engines Ltd, Glasgow.
12.6.1945: Launched by A. and J. Inglis Ltd., Glasgow, (Yard No.1301P), for the Ministry of War Transport, (British Tanker Company Ltd, managers). 9.10.1945: Completed. 1946: Owners restyled as the Ministry of Transport, (Anglo-Saxon Petroleum Company Ltd, appointed as managers). 1950: Coastal Tankers Ltd, appointed as managers. 1952: Sold to F.T. Everard and Sons Ltd, London, and renamed ALIGNITY. 18.11.1971: Hughes, Bolckow Ltd, commenced demolition at Blyth.

IRANIAN TANKER COMPANY LTD.

IRANIA (1929 - 1937)
O.N. 161218. 2,281g. 1,199n. 275.4 x 44.2 x 19.9 feet. Tanker.
3-cyl. 2 S.C.D.A. (545 x 965mm) 1,250 bhp Burns type oil engine
manufactured by Richardsons, Westgarth and Company Ltd, Hartlepool.
30.11.1928: Launched by Blythswood Shipbuilding Company Ltd,
Scotstoun (Yard No.21), for the Iranian Tanker Company Ltd
(Immingham Agency Company Ltd, managers), London. 4.1929:
Completed. 1937: Sold to Skibs. A/S Irania (H. Hannevig, manager),
Norway. During W.W.2, was under German control. 1948: Transferred to
A/S H. Hannevig, (E.C. Hannevig, manager), Norway, and renamed
ELIZABETH MARY. 1954: Sold to Borre D/S A/S, Norway. 1954: Sold to
F.T. Everard and Sons Ltd, London, and renamed ASTRALITY. 1954: Sold
to Fret-Maroc S.A. (Compagnie d'Armemente de Navires Citernes,
managers), Morocco, and renamed FRIMAU. 1957: Sold to Gem
Shipping Company, Honduras, and renamed MONT KETO. 1957: Sold to
Compagnie d'Armement Maritime, France, and renamed OBOCK. 1958:
Sold to C. Diamantis, Greece, and renamed THESSALONIKA. 1959: Sold
to Greek Tankership Company Ltd, Greece. 22.11.1963: Whilst on a
ballast voyage from Thessalonika to Pireaus, grounded on Euboea
Island, at a position 38.41 N 24.03 E. 7.12.1963: Her bow was sunk in 8'
of water whilst her stern was sunk in 30' of water with heavy bottom
damage, and declared a total loss.

IRANIA

ESPLEN TRUST LTD.

ET.1. SPRINGCRAG (1951 - 1954)
O.N. 168183. 332g. 153n. 130.2 x 25.2 x 9.0 feet.
Post 1977: 329g. 145n.
6-cyl. 2 S.C.S.A. (265 x 345mm) 330 bhp oil engine manufactured by Crossley Bros Ltd, Manchester.
15.3.1941: Launched as EMPIRE CRAG by J. Pollock, Son and Company Ltd, Faversham (Yard No. 1777), for the Ministry of War Transport (T.J. Metcalf Ltd, managers). 6.1941: Completed. 1943: Springwell Shipping Company Ltd, appointed managers. 23.3.1946: Purchased by Springwell Shipping Company Ltd, and renamed SPRINGCRAG. 1951: Purchased by the Esplen Trust Ltd (Springwell Shipping Company Ltd, managers). 1954: Sold to Walford Lines Ltd, London, and renamed WALCRAG. 1962: Sold to J.J. Prior (Transport) Ltd, London, and renamed COLNE TRADER. 1975: Sold to G.C. Yell and A.W. Nelson, London, and renamed SPITHEAD TRADER, for conversion into a crane ship. 1977: Sold to George Charles Yell, London. Still in service.

ET.2. RED SEA (1952 - 1953)
O.N. 147915. 640g. 289n. 175.3 x 27.6 x 11.0 feet.
T.3-cyl. (14", 23" & 38" x 27") 505 ihp engine manufactured by Aitchison, Blair Ltd, Clydebank.
19.8.1924: Launched as GEM by Scott and Sons, Bowling (Yard No.295), for Wm. Robertson, Glasgow. 8.1924: Completed. 1949: Transferred to Wm. Robertson (Shipowners) Ltd. 1952: Sold to the Esplen Trust Ltd, and renamed RED SEA, registered at Sunderland. 1953: Sold to Lindean Steam Ship Company Ltd, (G.T. Gillie and Blair Ltd, managers), and renamed GLENAPP CASTLE. 1958: Sold to Deeside Shipping Company Ltd (Thomas Rose and Company, managers), Sunderland and renamed DEESIDE. 11.1959: Sold to N/V De Koophandel, for demolition at Nieuwe Lekkerkerk. 3.1960: Work commenced.

ET.3. CEPOLIS (1955) see ship No. C.8.

RED SEA, as GEM

(WSPL)

CLAREMONT SHIPPING COMPANY LTD.

CL.1. CLAREPARK (1947)
O.N. 169816. 7,287g. 4,450n.   423.9 x 57.0 x 34.8 feet.
T.3-cyl. (24½", 37" & 70" x 48")   2,500 ihp engine manufactured by General Machinery Corp., Hamilton, Ontario.
13.1.1944: Launched as SAMEARN by the New England Shipbuilding Corp., East Yard, Portland, Maine (Yard No.2214), for the United States War Shipping Administration. 2.1944: Completed and bareboat chartered to the Ministry of War Transport (Houlder Brothers and Company Ltd, managers), London. 17.4.1947: Sold to the Claremont Shipping Company Ltd (Immingham Agency Company Ltd, managers), London, and renamed CLAREPARK. 20.4.1947: Management reverted to Houlder Brothers and Company Ltd.   1950: Sold to Argosam Shipping Company Ltd (A. Lusi Ltd, managers), London, and renamed ARGOLIB. 1956: Sold to West Africa Navigation Ltd, Liberia, and renamed AFRICAN PRINCESS. 12.6.1968: Arrived at Kaohsiung for demolition. 8.1968: Work commenced.

CLAREMONT in Houlder Line colours   *(A. Duncan)*

108

LEADENHALL SHIPPING COMPANY LTD.

LS.1. LEASPRAY (1952 - 1956) see ship No. C.3.

LS.2. LEAFOAM (1953)
O.N.183177. 552g. 255n. 168.3 x 30.1 x 8.2 feet.
8-cyl. 2 S.C.S.A. (265 x 345mm) 480 bhp oil engine manufactured in 1945 by Crossley Bros Ltd, Manchester.
Originally one of four 160 feet, twin screw auxiliary vessels ordered by the Admiralty (Fleet Air Arm) from J. Pollock, Sons and Company Ltd. Faversham, for the purpose of ferrying aircraft and aviation stores between aircraft carriers and shore establishments. To have been named SEA GLADIATOR this order was cancelled in 1947 and the partly constructed hull sold to E.J. and W. Goldsmith Ltd, London, radically rebuilt, converted to single engine and lengthened by 8 feet. 24.9.1949: Launched as GOLDLYNX by J. Pollock, Sons and Company Ltd, Faversham (Yard No.1845), for E.J. and W. Goldsmith, London. 2.1950: Completed. 1951: Sold to Springwell Shipping Company Ltd, London, and renamed SPRINGWOOD. 1953: Sold to Leadenhall Shipping Company Ltd, London, and renamed LEAFOAM. 1953: Sold to John Kelly Ltd (J.G. Christie, manager), Belfast, and renamed BALLYEDWARD. 1955: E.W.P. King appointed manager. 1970: John Kelly Wilson appointed manager. 1970: Sold to Zodiac Shipping Company Ltd, Newry, and renamed LADY HYACINTH. 1973: Sold by public auction at Rouen, to European Ferries Ltd, Dublin, and renamed GOLDEN TRADER (Registered at Manchester). 1973: Owners restyled as Commercial Ferries Ltd. 1974: Sold for demolition at Gijon.

LEASPRAY   *(WSPL)*

SPRINGWOOD

HYDRAGALE, ex WALRUS

SEAFOX   (Wright & Logan)

CONVERSION FOR PEACE

Overnight the end of World War II in 1945 made ships redundant. Many warships were cancelled before construction had commenced and others on the building berths were scrapped in situ. Material on hand was diverted to projects with a peacetime priority and the redesign of hulls suitable for commercial employment received attention as it allowed early delivery of ships to fill needs created by the loss of vessels in the war.

Amongst the ships on order in the summer of 1945 was a group of seven naval aviation store carriers, designed to carry aircraft and act as attendants for large aircraft carriers. With a length overall of 172 feet and a beam of 30 feet they were powered by twin Crossley diesels giving 960 bhp and a speed of 10.5 kts. The names chosen for them commemmorated aircraft.

Three ordered from the Blyth Shipbuilding and Dry Docks Company Ltd, Blyth, were delivered in 1945/46 as BLACKBURN, ROC and WALRUS, as were the first two from James Pollock, Sons and Company Ltd, Faversham, named RIPON and SEA FOX. The other Pollock ships, SEA GLADIATOR and SEA HURRICANE, were cancelled.

'The Motor Ship' (April 1948) contained an account and before / after drawings relating to SEA GLADIATOR and SEA HURRICANE. The partially completed hulls were purchased by E.J. & W. Goldsmith Ltd, and underwent radical redesign to emerge as single screw, raised quarterdeck coasters with bridge aft and a cruiser stern replacing the flat naval transom. One main engine was retained, which at 480 bhp gave a service speed of 9 kts. Completed in 1948/49 they were given the names GOLDLYNX (see ship LS.2 above) and GOLDHIND (see ship C.6).

All five delivered to the Royal Navy were sold into commercial service, commencing in 1958. BLACKBURN and WALRUS were converted for the offshore oil industry and served at various times as survey and drilling ships. ROC, RIPON and SEA FOX became cargo ships and traded in many areas of the world, including North America, the Caribbean, Australasia, India and the Persian Gulf.

Comparison of the picture of SEA FOX, taken in April 1947, with SPRINGWOOD (ex GOLDLYNX) gives no hint of their common ancestry.

IMMINGHAM AGENCY COMPANY LTD

WARWICK AND ESPLEN LTD

Name	Appointed	Resigned
Chairmen:		
M.C. Houlder	18. 9.1912	19. 9.1924
W.C. Warwick	19. 9.1924	31. 1.1962
W. Graham Esplen	1. 2.1962	31.12.1970
C.W. Warwick	3. 3.1971	14. 7.1985*
P.J. Warwick	14. 7.1985	current
Directors:		
M.C. Houlder	18. 9.1912	19. 9.1924
W.C. Warwick	18. 9.1912	31. 1.1962
S.H. Kaye	18. 9.1912	19. 9.1924
J.P. Harper	18. 9.1912	25.10.1918
W. Graham Esplen	19. 2.1924	7. 4.1947
(later Sir Graham Esplen)	1.10.1952	31.12.1967
C.L. Warwick	19. 9.1924	31. 7.1938
	10. 4.1945	30. 9.1969
James Huntly	16. 5.1938	30. 9.1957
	1. 2.1962	7.12.1977*
C.W. Warwick	4. 8.1938	14. 7.1985*
J.E. Chase	1.10.1957	30. 9.1969
John G. Esplen	1. 2.1962	31. 1.1971
P.J. Warwick	1. 2.1962	current
P.F.S. Kittermaster	1.10.1969	12.11.1971
A.H.E. Hood	15.12.1971	current
Mrs A.M. Hood	1.10.1976	current
Mrs M.J. Warwick	1.10.1976	current
J.W.F. Warwick	1.10.1992	current
Secretaries:		
J.P. Harper	18. 9.1912	25.10.1918
L.P. Sheldon	25.10.1918	21.10.1937*
J.E. Chase	25.10.1937	1.10.1957**
J.B. Hood	1.10.1957	18.12.1974
A.H.E. Hood	18.12.1974	1.11.1992
J.W. Stanford	1.11.1992	current

* date deceased, all other dates are of resignation or retirement.

** resigned as secretary on being appointed a director.

HADLEY SHIPPING COMPANY LTD

Name	Appointed	Resigned
Chairmen:		
W.C. Warwick	18.12.1926	1. 2.1962
C.W. Warwick	1. 2.1962	14. 3.1985
P.J. Warwick	14. 3.1985	current
Directors:		
W.C. Warwick	18.12.1926	31. 1.1962
Sir John Esplen, Bt	18.12.1926	7. 2.1930*
W. Graham Esplen	18.12.1926	31.12.1970
(later Sir Graham Esplen)		
C.L. Warwick	18.12.1926	30. 9.1969
Sir James Caird, Bt	24. 2.1930	26. 7.1949
James Huntly	20. 4.1938	7.12.1977*
C.W. Warwick	1. 8.1938	14. 3.1985
J.M. Houlder	14. 2.1947	current
J.E. Chase	1. 2.1962	30. 9.1969
John G. Esplen	1. 2.1962	22.10.1973
P.J. Warwick	1. 2.1962	current
P.F.S. Kittermaster	1.10.1969	12.11.1971
A.H.E. Hood	15.12.1971	current
M.F. Puttnam	1. 1.1973	30. 6.1989
J.D. Brown	23.11.1973	current
J.M. Reid	1. 2.1977	19.12.1983
J.W.F. Warwick	1.10.1992	current
Secretaries:		
A.W. Hobbs	18.12.1926	1. 7.1948
J.E. Chase	1. 7.1948	16. 3.1962
J.B. Hood	16. 3.1962	18.12.1974
A.H.E. Hood	18.12.1974	1.11.1992
J.W. Stanford	1.11.1992	current

* date deceased, all other dates are of resignation or retirement.

** resigned as secretary on being appointed a director.

'CERINTHUS' REMEMBERED

Donald Bullock joined the CERINTHUS as sixth engineer in 1955, and served continuously on the ship for 10 years until he was forced to leave, having suffered severe burns whilst on board. When he recovered he went back to sea in other Houlder ships, but in 1973 he returned to CERINTHUS as Second Engineer. He finally left the ship in July 1976 when she was sold to shipbreakers.

He put his recollections of life on CERINTHUS into the following verses:

The Cerinthus is the bonniest ship
That ever went down to the sea
She's been around on wave and ground
Since 1953.

I first clapped eyes on the lovely lass
When I was a wet eared lad,
As a junior then I sailed with men
Who'd seen her ribs in the yard.

She was clothed in the highest class of steel
That the shipwright's art had seen
And tho' wear and tear have rubbed her bare,
Her form's still that of a Queen.

We've sailed around the world's sea lanes
Have my old girl and me,
From Ecuador to Singapore
and Hong Kong to the Caribee.

In November of 1958
We were Anacortes bound
When the turbine thrust gave up the ghost
and the Water wall fell down.

At Miri town the work was done
Old Horsburgh flew out
And Bomber came to learn the game
"I'll fix it!" was the shout.

The time flew by with mindless heed
As onward East we sailed
But Tallulah's gin had drained the bin
And hunger made us quail.

"Fear not, brave lads" Frank said to us
"Think of the money I'm saving!"
But cornflakes and stale oatcakes
Is not a diet I'm craving.

114

CERINTHUS after arrival at Faslane on 2 July 1976 for breaking up. Alongside is EL LOBO which had arrived on 29 June

(G. Gardner)

I deserted her in '59
to try my luck ashore
But my old friend was in need of a mend
When I came back in '64.

The vaps were up to their usual tricks
And both smoke glasses were black,
Then she vented her spite one Sunday night
And took the skin off my back.

Old snowy and Fred got quite a fright.
And put me ashore in St Croix,
So for nine long years I shed no tears
Over what she had done to her boy.

And then one day a panic arose
"We've no relief for the second".
So in '73 they sent for me
And her grimy gangway beckoned.

I've sailed on board her twice since then
And she keeps on getting better.
For you learn to thole a ship with a soul,
If she wants to burble, you let her.

But now depression days have come
The tanker trade's gone sour
And Joe Shell says we've got to pay
With this old friend of ours.

They'll break you up, and me as well
At Faslane on the Clyde,
So when you've done your final run,
Good-Bye Old ship o'mine.

Donald B. Bullock

115

FLAGS AND FUNNELS

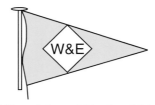

Warwick and Esplen Ltd

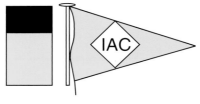

*Immingham Agency
Company Ltd*

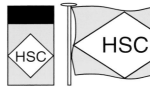

*Hadley Shipping
Company Ltd*

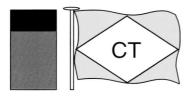

Coastal Tankers Ltd

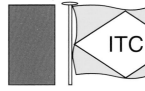

*Iranian Tankers
Company Ltd*

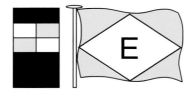

Esplen Trust Ltd

*Leadenhall Shipping
Company Ltd*

PICTORIAL ADDENDUM

As this book went to press a selection of photographs was received, some of which are reproduced on this and subsequent pages.

CLYDESDALE after being launched by Mrs Margaret Warwick. She received a bouquet from the youngest apprentice in the shipyard with her husband, Peter Warwick, looking on (James Weir)

CORATO (3) being launched at Foxhol by Mrs Eileen Chase. Her husband, James Chase (secretary 1948-62 and director 1962-9) is at her right hand
(Fotobedrijf Piet Boonstra)

CORATO (2) on trials. The launch party (below, left to right) Captain Allen, unknown, unknown, Mrs Huntly, Mrs Chase, Mr Morrison, Mr Chase, Sir Graham Esplen, Mr Huntly, Captain Melville, Mr & Mrs Horsbrough.

Mrs Angela Hood sponsored CERINTHUS (4), named afloat at Appledore in 1978. With her is the daughter of a shipyard worker who presented the bouquet and Mr Ball, Chairman of the builders.

Sir John Esplen (see page 15)

INDEX

Elkhound (2) proposed		CM.4.
Else		CM.29.
EMPIRE AMETHYST		HM.2.
EMPIRE BAIRN		
EMPIRE BUTE		CM.22.
EMPIRE COMMERCE		HM.5.
EMPIRE COPPICE		CM.4.
Empire Crag		ET.1.
EMPIRE CROSS		HM.13.
Empire Estuary		C.5.
EMPIRE FAUN		CM.3.
EMPIRE FITZROY		CM.41.
EMPIRE GAIN		HM.6.
EMPIRE GRANITE		HM.1.
EMPIRE HARP	CM.2.	CM.38.
EMPIRE JEWEL	HM.10	CM.27.
EMPIRE JUMNA		HM.7.
EMPIRE JURA		CM.21.
EMPIRE MAIDEN		CM.1.
Empire Mars		HM.16.
Empire Milner		HM.17.
EMPIRE PIKE		CM.26.
EMPIRE SHETLAND		CM.40.
EMPIRE SIMBA		HM.4.
EMPIRE TADPOLE		CM.25.
EMPIRE TAGINDA		HM.9.
EMPIRE TAGRALIA		HM.11.
EMPIRE TEGAYA		CM.36.
EMPIRE TEGEDEN		HM.8.
EMPIRE TEGLEONE		HM.12.
EMPIRE TEGYIKA		CM.30.
EMPIRE TIGINA		CM.29.
EMPIRE TIGONTO		CM.27.
EMPIRE TIGOUVER		CM.28.
Empire Tulip		C.6.
Eternity Venture		H.23.
Evdokia II		H.13.
Feolent		HM.8.
Fiddown		C.5.
Fiskela		H.15.
Five Star		H.11.
Flag Paola		H.16.
Foca		CM.33.
FORT ST.PAUL		HM.15.
Fossarus	HM.10	CM.27.
Fossularca		HM.7.
Franco Lisi		CM.36.
Frimau		IT.1.
Frisia		HC.1.
Gem		ET.2.
General Zawadzki		H.24.
General Mitchell Baker		CM.11.
Glenapp Castle		ET.2.
Golden Trader		LS.2.
GOLDDRIFT		C.3.
GOLDEVE		C.4.
GOLDFAUN		C.5.
GOLDGNOME		C.6.
GOLDHIND		C.7.
Goldlynx		LS.2.
Grande		CM.14.
Gran		CM.14.
Green Rock		H.17.
Grete		CM.28.
Gulf Kestrel		H.11.
Gustaf Heinrich Weitert		HC.1.
Hanna		CM.32.
Harco		H.14.
HASTINGS		CM.24.
Helny		CM.16.
HILDE		CM.32.
Ho Ping 50		HM.15.
Ho Ping Wu Shi		HM.15.
Ile De Montreal		CM.25.
Insistence		C.6.
IRANIA		IT.1.
Izrada		HM.3.
JAMAICA PLANTER		H.5.
Jantje R.	ET.3	C.3.
Jerba		H.19.
Jeverland		HM.8.
Julius Schindler		CM.36.
Kali Limenes II		HM.12.
Kama	ET.3	C.3.
Kamran		CM.14.
Kamuni		CM.15.
Kennerleya		HM.1.
Klaver		CM.11.
Kyllini		CM.30.
L'Ardeche		CM.31.
Lady Hyacinth		LS.2.
Lake Charles		CM.6.
LEAFOAM		LS.2.
LEASPRAY		LS.1.
Liselotte Essberger		CM.30.
Loc Bay		CM.6.
Longford		HM.15.
Lucia 2		CM.9.
Luki		H.6.
Magd		HM.6.
Marcello Garolla		CM.21.
Marcello G.		CM.21.
Maria		CM.12.
Maria Rosa		CM.16.
Marika		HM.15.
Maro		CM.20.
Marsteinen		HM.12.
Marxburg		HC.1.
Masahi		C.7.
Mashona		CM.19.
Mashona Coast		CM.19.
Mata K		H.21.
Max Albrecht		HM.11.
Maya		HC.1.
Mercurius		CM.17.
Miliana		CM.22.
Milo		CM.13.
Minaa Maaree		C.7.